SPEAK FROM HERE TO THERE

TWO POEM CYCLES

ACKNOWLEDGEMENTS

Poems 93 ("We arrive early at the soirée"), 100 ("What we say is where we say") and 105 ("I've been searching the sky") first appeared in the *Boston Review*.

SPEAK FROM HERE TO THERE

TWO POEM CYCLES

BY

KWAME DAWES AND JOHN KINSELLA

P E E P A L   T R E E

First published in Great Britain in 2016
Peepal Tree Press Ltd
17 King's Avenue
Leeds LS6 1QS
UK

ISBN 13: 9781845233198

Supported using public funding by
**ARTS COUNCIL
ENGLAND**

INDEX OF FIRST LINES

In Cycle One, all the odd-numbered poems are by John Kinsella (JK) and all the even numbers by Kwame Dawes (KD). In Cycle Two, all the even numbers are by John Kinsella and all the odd numbers by Kwame Dawes.

Cycle One
Speak from Here...
Echoes and Refrains

Cycle Two
… To There
Illuminations

CYCLE ONE

Speak from Here…

Echoes and Refrains

1.

We co-exist. The York gum bark is stripping itself off,
shiny skin underneath exposed to the sun. Late summer –
summers that won't end – and it seems to be a statement,
much more than restating a habit, a well-researched fact.
Tim is home-schooled by Tracy who is making a full-time
job of it. He goes to the city for sports once a week.
We co-exist. But the rest of the district is closed off.
Though animals and birds pass through and we say hello.

JK

2.

The late actor's wife,
the famous poet,
lectures me humbly
on the etymology of hubris –

All Greek to me, she says.
Nothing in our dialect
for it – by "our",
she means, generously,

America, though here
in deep winter,
I walk my cockapoo
under the gentle tyranny

of the prideful
humility of the Midwest –
a collective hubris.

My daughter calls
from another city,
crying for her loneliness,
but laughing at the absurdity of it.

Together we wonder
where we will build a kraal
for our clan, with its own boneyard
for our scattered dead.

KD

3.

We live on the boodja of the Noongah people. We are actually
at the crossroads of three tribes. South from here, the Avon river
used to flood but it's been trained out of its old shape.
We don't see ourselves as owning, but keep the scramble bikes
and rifles out. Trees planted, an effort to restore the bush.
Gestures? Tim was driven from school by the children of neo-Nazis.
Literally. Out in the bush, they run concentration camps in their heads —
not yet ripe enough to export, but with their home-grown flavour.

JK

4.

Another quarrel
with my father-in-law.

I speak but my wife carries
the heat in her.

We won't buy the strip of land
he wants to collect,

all stone and acacia
in the hills over Kingston.

I am trapped in the middle
of generations of neglected promises.

But he knows the land well.
His grandmother kept her slavey name

while she lived as a gatherer
of herbs and insects to heal

the ailing and curse the prideful.
She never drove in a car

and climbed breadfruit trees
when she was eighty.

If only her oil-green fingers
could heal the sores in our Anancy ways.

KD

5.

I look for healing in music but the seeing and listening are confused.
Between the notes of all genres I hear the colonial whispering: theft theft.
Tim was born in America. Americans claim him as American. Of the soil.
I am not sure whose soil. But Tim listens to Son House and Robert Johnson
and tells me there are truths in there meant for him to hear. He is twelve.
He has pictures of them on his wall. He told me today he's heading for Memphis
as soon as he can. There's something there for him to find. But he loves
the parrots and echidnas and kangaroos here. He loves our conversations.

JK

6.

I am a lazy thinker –
it was not always this way.
Once, I relished the pain
of thought. I waded into

the impossible equations of home
and wrote a book
with the hubris of one who knows.

These days, I walk with Hopkins's poplars
scattered over British soil in my head,
and I feel a deep sadness,

not for the land stripped bare –
all seared with toil and all that jazz –
but for the man, lonely and full

of untasted lust for the farrier,
bent over, broken. These days,
home is the small space

between Lorna and me,
how we fill it with meaning,
and hack our way through the undergrowth
of betrayals, a path enough for hope.

KD

7.

I always clean the bottom of my boots before travelling – to make sure
I carry no soil pathogens from one zone to another. It comes from living
in a dieback region where a single spore might bring down a forest of trees
and metaphors. But I don't think like that outside reality. I don't make analogies
or fear travelling to "far-from-home" places. I have spent a life on the road,
but less so now. It's still life. And I am well-suited to staring at a square inch
of dirt for hours – watching the ants crawl over the grand narratives that feed
this "isolation", amuse myself with a late, revivified surrealism that has
nothing to do with images and everything to do with denying the ballot box.

JK

8.
Even if I feel the sun on my skin, every day, if...

— Ibeyi "Oya"

And now the flurries...

Yesterday I thought of the solstice,
the hope of brighter days ahead — for once it comforted me,

which is how I know my body
is making home in alien places, again.

You say you seek healing in music.
I say the eyes of those two Cuban sisters,
Ibeyi, carry the elegant guile
of Oyá, a certain haunting, and their voices:
such frightful beauty in their harmonizing!

The snow will cover everything —
then there will be an interim of silence.

KD

9.

This helps me to piece things together. This, your inner-
mosts and exteriors, your quotidians and special insights.
In the solipsism of the bush, they are input and more —
the snow falling on your day counterpoints the ash
of burnt offerings that has coated the denials of here,
your silence muffles the crack of a bullet detonating
against the complex foliage that bulldozers would take
out if we didn't resist. The whole lot, vanquished.
I've been translating some of Petrarch's *Rime sparse*
expanding memory's parameters, the dead of summer.

JK

10.
"Revolutionary to rass!"
— Ivan, *The Harder They Come*

For two days
I have thought to mention Kamau B,

mouth juiced with pawpaw
in his shady backyard in Barbados,
ticking out on a syrup-sticky laptop
his last elegant elegies,

perpetually in lament
for a dead wife,
a burnt-out archive,
and Cow Pasture,
that ancestral burial ground
where he once photographed
a spirit (lost to developers and nefarious deed),

and how he now wishes he had drawn for his 'las
and caused sweet carnage.

KD

11.

Exfoliation of granite, the strewn stones of Coondle.
All those losses covered up by homogenous record-keepers.
Islands by degrees, islands accumulating as gold mines
where grandmother provided ghost-signs: remembering
where the bread was baked and who baked it, where
the shafts flooded far down under a sky that only broke
open once every three years. Inland. A desert of lament.
Or far from here, across the Indian ocean, the lava-flows
of the Piton de la Fournaise, the eating of Piton-Sainte-Rose,
a sidereal gesture as the dark field smokes your feet.

JK

12.

What is the word for the sweet pain
for things dreamed, imagined
or longed for in the future –

nothing abstract, but whole as the accumulation of need:
a daily orange-yolked egg, thick hot cocoa,
chunks of hardo bread, a long glass of milk,
oil-soaked ackee and firm slivers of stewed cabbage –
and more, dawn light, a desk, and the murmur of the sea?

What is the word for shame, when Coptic labourers kneel,
waiting for their crude beheading under garish movie lights
and the anointment of a zealot's prayers?

KD

13.

I lose track but rarely of where I am. Today, late afternoon
when the UV has lost some of its bite, I walk with Tim along
the main street of Northam. It is entirely blank other than
a couple of kids pulling stunts on skateboards. Then a car jags
the corner next to the Weston Flour Mill, with a cop cruiser
on its bumper. Tim knows to keep his eyes to the ground, to look
anywhere but at the "incident", because it will make things
volatile. I watch out the corner of my eye, just to keep track –
always the witness, a force of habit. But then, pink and grey
galahs rush the main street to rectify states of absence.

JK

14.

T'row down your arms and come
                    — Burning Spear

I have adopted
the antic joviality
of a priest

with spit-muddy fingers
to cover eyelids brown
before the expletive:

Be healed! And the trees
are without leaves,
the sky a stony grey,

but someone is dancing
wild-eyed in the snow.
My water-table of tears

is shallow these days,
and news of bloody
genocides

or the inconveniences
of failed love make me cry
like a blubbering shaman.

KD

15.

I stopped looking over my shoulder when I knew
there was something there to look at. But I don't forget
what I passed, and the strains of bands shaking up
town halls still resonate. When I cut my dreadlocks
and shed them to the forest – the police on the outskirts
sniffing the air for contraband – I abandoned the bus
wreck on the road to Kathmandu, the residues
burning far below. Falling between the mountains,
choking on Yak cigarettes, I renounced without
an echo. Is this what Keith Richards calls "weaving"?

JK

16.

Another John, a poet from St. Lucia with its Pitons,
discarded, too, his dreadlocks, confessing to the breddrin
at the ital grounation his sudden tumbling into Babylon's
light – Damascus and all. I envy him the shedding of righteous
barefooted austerity for the Jesus thing – glory to glory.
Me? I came from cynic squalor, from muddy baldhead
to crazy baldhead. The comrades lamented my madness
as they left me bewildered and trembling in the backwoods.

KD

17.

In the span of a hand, ochre blown around to sign rockface
encyclopaedia, uranium and gas fields, the petroglyph
transportation – how is this conveyed? Three days in excess
of 42C (Napoleon's empire building as precise as civics),
or 108-plus in imperial (which speaks for itself – I cross
the generations of change), though even before, retreating
south from the flaming hot weather, even hotter now, down
to the granite cliffs facing the Antarctic which falls to pieces
mid-conversation, the bark has pulled away from the upper
branches of the York gums as it does each year: they gleam!

JK

18.
After Tarkovsky's "Andrei Rublev"
        For Basuli Deb

From here,
on this side of the river,
after the mad flight
over the horde of executioners,

after the wild laughter
of one who thinks he has gotten away,
the news arrives
that the reinforcements
do not fear water
and they take
no prisoners;

the news comes
that the death we thought
we had escaped is upon us.

There is nothing more sorrowful
than the end of battles
while the gloating victors
look on. This is all metaphor
for the petty politics
of race in civil universities –
an indulgence, no doubt.

But it matters still
that a small Indian woman
is packing her future,
deported by this monstrous machine.

America neither sweats nor blusters – so clinical we miss the blood.

KD

19.

It's often zone-talk I am caught up in, as when a sudden change
of plans wrenched Tracy from her Russian-language studies
and an osprey took up residence on a phone tower, changing
the status quo of its brain chemistry. I am working on a libretto
for yet another version of Faust – there can never be too many.
The stress in renewing a visa so one can regain entry into
the country where my son was born defies the anti-nuclear
Reaganite red rag to a bull, the sound and the fury and the cells
of a lock-up from which I watched a Noongah kid get beaten to death
by boys in blue who formed a circle of trust, a new medieval.

JK

20.

These short chapters –
the drawing room rituals
of Tolstoy's nobles –

one can't miss the under-stench
of the rotting dead,
the shallow graves.

In a film the twenty-year old bones
of a family fit inside a woollen blanket
which they carry across a bleak country
for reburial – the holes that were their eyes.

Lorna and I sit in the silver mist
of a Nebraska dawn,
the car still cupping us warmly;

we are buffeted in with coats and scarfs,
and we imagine the chopping
of the bodies of a man and his wife in Bangladesh;

we wonder who'd we deny
before we howl at the intent
of the cleaver pressed into our throats?

KD

21.

Just read this news. I know that city well. Was there in 1985, lost for weeks on New Elephant Road, then the river. The war still ran the city, those many years later – shell-shocked buildings offering little shelter, x-ray equipment exposed to the weather without any lead shielding. The day I arrived with a backpack pushing a ridiculous rhythm, I found myself forced to step over the swollen corpse of a starved child. I read local poets translated into English and pieced myself into a picture in which I had no belonging. Insinuated, I see now. Just read the news. There are flowers where he fell. I saw flowers strewn everywhere. I heard the prayers from the minarets. The poetry was strong and spoke nowhere of killing, spoke nowhere of cutting out the breath.

JK

23.

Storm coming in so it's a matter of getting this out before the shutdown.
Yesterday we journeyed to Yarloop where I once ran with then girlfriend
and brother, all in our early 20s, escaping "the scene". "Dairy country" – where
watching cows drag a timewarp around had me a vegan within weeks.
With my brother and two others we worked the haycarting – rural labour
long being my fallback. Under the clouds of toxic fumes from the Alcoa
refinery, the hills being stripped of forest and bauxite, I plotted a course
into a future which zigzagged its way through chaos. Cause and effect. We
couldn't stay long in the old timber town because of the fallout. Marri
trees were in blossom and wooden houses had been given a lick of paint.

JK

24.

It is, then, as if there are doors
leading into doors into doors,
a complex of rooms of shelter
that go as deep into memory,
grey and sculpted as light will allow.
The domestic negotiations
of affection and desire continue
until we sleep like labourers,
a deep consuming sleep.
Tonight I hovered over us
and found the depth of our sleep alarming:
how easily we forgot each other!
Then we woke to the news
of a slaughtered politician
and I wanted to ask you
if you were thinking of his girlfriend
sobbing at dawn, not once thinking
of protests or intrigue. *He listened to me*
like a woman, she said.
In Russia doors close around the deep sleepers.

KD

25.

A poet friend of mine in Moscow speaks of the poetry community
as "atomised" and "gone to ground". We know that wifi is the asbestos
of tomorrow. I am becoming like my son and compiling lists. For
some reason I can't get out of my head an incident that happened –
took place? – in the mid-90s... Jack, this tough guy I knew who held
the opposite politics to me... the opposite, my contra in every way,
I'd say..., was shot five times by a dealer or someone he'd ripped-off...
five times outside a suburban shopping centre running from an ATM –
left to die in the car park. He was a skinhead from the north of England –
a furious bigot who loathed everything I stood for, but nonetheless
when he saw me being beaten in a city hotel, stepped in and stopped
my attacker in his tracks with, "Fooken touch 'im, mate, and yool fooken
unsa to me!" Never forgotten it, Jack. Thanks. These surfacings.

JK

26.

for Kamau Brathwaite

It is as if there is a shadow
of something whole

interrupting the relentless clouds
of snow swirling about us,

and suddenly, the dark body
of steel, wood and canvas,

sailing through with the warm laughter
of a singing troupe drunk

with careless delight,
becomes everything in the world.

This is how the news
that Kamau Brathwaite had won

the medal named after that tricky,
tricky New Hampshire poet,

who sardonically goaded
his earnest best friend to war,

after those walking talks on well-worn
paths across the endless English fields

arrived here in Lincoln in late winter,
the interruption of gloom with holy news.

But no matter, Kamau,
who is all kindness and light,

asked me a month ago
the truest translation of Kokroko,

and there was that truck
hurtling through the blizzard

and those Akan voices singing,
Big God, Mighty God,

Kokroko, Kokroko,
in holy astonishment.

KD

27.

Interruption, though I carried the snow with me through the heat
of yesterday down into the city to where the river curves past
Applecross Jetty and Point Dundas – Moondaap – where a week
ago a World War One grenade was hauled from the river, a white-
faced heron treading hesitantly towards the disrupted source.
In gathering words in clusters and expressions, a language
is being reconstituted. A nereid in the garden of a new mansion
stretches out and stares into a leaf-shaped pool, her bronzed skin
deflecting the glare off the river. She looks blissfully absorbed
in her reflection. And then we learn Tracy has to be taken as fast
as possible to the hospital, and the country tumbles down the Scarp
and I sit late as victims of night violence are taken into emergency.

JK

28.

Put a child in a train
and cover him
with the silence of heat,

then in an emergency
of percussive clanks,
let a factory line of tanks

shudder past him –
this after the sun has grown
eggy over the hills.

Put a girl with a shaved head
in the shade
of a banana tree

and let her stare
at the blue-grey
of machetes lined up

for yards and yards
like soldiers
before the chaos of blood.

Teach a child
the economics of death.
Let her know

that whiskey mutes
all tenderness
and music will grow

a caul over all wounds,
ugly as the embossment
of keloids.

Let her learn to sleep
until she wakes.
This morning I dismiss

these dreams,
but the one
that is a question lingers:

What you said
of Tracy and hospitals,
how present is the tense?

KD

29.

The tense is present – tension an irony this heart can't resolve.
To monitor the chambers as dreams mess with mortality, and they
watch the ECGs and flows of experience making irregular art. But
all around, the wounds not yet scars of other lives crossed in triage.
I am in Aimé Césaire's *Cahier d'un retour au pays natal*, writing
my own in the car under the carpark demi-lights, just near where
getting out I spiked myself on a native grass tree, and think over
past joys making the present a misery; but it's not like that really:
listening to the whispering deaths of a late night "metal music"
programme, and the jokes of growling prophecy, a guy slumped
from an OD and cops bringing their offerings in and out. And
then I'm in, and Tracy is still wired and we smile through it all
and then we are "debout sous les étoiles" with all we've shared.

JK

30.

Here then are the stones
to build a shrine to what we do not know.

Here are the dried leaves
for the pyre to send up smoke
to God for the dead.

It is true that what I have seen of violence
has been so swift, so casual, so much a part
of the body's shape that it seems
I have lived a charmed life,
that I do not know what violence is.

It is how we survive, I suppose, though even
that word seems a lie.

The bombs in Nigeria, the clumsy
improvisations of killers –
they are the interruptions of a green forest,
then the blood, the torn garments,
the uncertain details of the dead and wounded.
The weather has changed. Ah, stars!

It is time to shed the fat of winter – I will sweat again, amen.
I am now counting the days between sorrows, the hiatus
has been too long, the tossed bones say. This is no way to pray.

KD

31.

Processing works and days I come up against the stockpiles
of leisure and retribution sending us on our way. This is world,
they say, closing their ears to the music. Taj Mahal insists,
"The blues is a transformational miracle...", and I reckon
he's right. A juvenile gwardar slid past Tracy's bare foot
yesterday and lifted its head as she exclaimed and I watched
as it came towards me then veered away – a snake called "deadly",
but a snake that avoids contacts with humans. In its bands (there
are different configurations of colour and geometry in the skins
of gwardars) were the colours of dawn and sunset and an overcast
sky, the tail of the cyclone having come to us as a rain-bearing
depression – an ex-tropical cyclone dumping its residues
on the wheatbelt. And all this comes together now and for
you, too. We weave our way through; write a détente?

JK

32.

I am shadowed by what should be called the walking dream,
the one that won't let go, that arrives in between thought
unannounced. I welcomed a kind of haunting, but for me
it is the hiatus between your last poem and the next, it is
this thing of Tracy, the name we metered into our lines
as if I am waiting for fragments to clump together
in a pattern that makes sense. It has been days. And I am waiting
with a song about the warmth over the prairies now,
about the neighbour mowing tawny grass long before
the green has set in, as if marking the spot against
a late snowfall. We have no gwardars here, though our
adders are in the silences. There is a weight that comes with this,
this waiting for your music and its assurance of safety and light.

KD

33.

Yes, when a glimpse into other lives is offered, we become
part of them to greater or less degrees. Identity is made
from a brief conversation in the street, from years living
under the same roof. I have been with Tracy for almost 22 years,
but if we'd met as children we'd likely have built a future
out of what the other was doing. She's doing okay – waiting
for test results, and stoical as usual – it's the ex-Carmelite
postulant in her, but the portion mixed with the incredulities
of life shut off from the world. Today, I have been reading
of the Moore River Native Settlement and the pure evil
of the white colonial administrators who stole children
from Aboriginal woman because they were fathered by
white men, who took the kids far from their tribal lands
and interned them, farming them out as servants to white
families, and often clawing them back pregnant for two years
before removing their babies and sending these new mothers
back out as servants to other white families. The "protector"
of Aborigines A. O. Neville said, "Thus the children
grow up as whites, knowing nothing of their own people.
At the expiration of the two years the mother goes back
into service so it really doesn't matter if she has half-
a-dozen children." Identity. What really disturbs me
in telling you this is how easily the quotation lineates,
how horror can be parsed into the lyric and signed
off on. Tracy and I have been talking about this all
evening. It feels like you are present, talking it over –
angry with us. There must be restitution. The song
has to be returned to its rightful owners. And this
is beyond property – it goes to the heart of "country".

JK

34.

Time is its own gift that should be enough – that is the son,
gangly, muscles in his jaw, a beard tufting with revolutionary

insouciance – and the daughters upbraid him, while we are gathered
around the blue light of our little phones, a family of texters

contemplating twenty-five years of marriage – *Hahaha*, says Lorna,
hahaha, good one, and I think it is twenty-five years plus the ten

when we waited, drifting bodies, secure in the secret pact
of the day I shook, startled at my sudden mourning, while she alone

held me, as if afraid to let me fall – my father freshly dead;
for once there was no performance, no antic trauma.

I pity the fool who tries to sniff around her. She pities
the fool who dares to sniff around me – we have become

broken bones now fused together like this. Such is the unworthiness
of love or whatever this thing is. *Hahahaha*, I say. Let us

elope! Let us tell the secrets we fear will be told. Like Leo
Tolstoy casually cataloguing the secrets of the Free Masons,

whistle-blower or some disgruntled apostate, or are we, Leo
and us, merely building smokescreens, myths to throw

off the hunters? There is no question here – not really;
after all, the days have grown longer, and we find comfort

in the slight pressure of shin against calf, a kind of waltz
by seasoned veterans. Anger, John, is reserved for a special

class of inhumanity – the absence of imagination and the soft
music of empathy that should leave us damp with tears; anger

is reserved for the hypocrites, the parasites, and even then
there is reggae, a whistle clean like a whistle in the air:

Kill, vank and paralyze, all weak-heart conception
Wipe them out of creation, creation, wadada oh!

Ahh, Bob!

KD

35.

Ah, but Kwame, John Lydon, aka Johnny Rotten, tells us
that "anger is an energy"! Now, where's this committed long-

term pacifist to go with such a stock epithet? Younger, an addict,
I smothered violence in a cloud of obscurity, knowing anger

was a useless emotion, as good as abstract nouns. Now,
I turn the other cheek but speak loudly as I turn – it's not

quietist, but a channelling into plosive and fricatives,
stuck on adjectives of uprights and horizontals, trees

and creatures moving on through, the crazed flight angles
of pink & greys, the loops of ring-necked parrots. Romanticism

dropped dead in clarity, and I will resist surveillance and owner-
ship till the end, which will be as the passenger passing through.

There are plenty of mosquitoes here and I recognise their rights
to suck me dry – a bonanza of the proverbial unified self.

I am not much angry with them, or anyone personally.
But I do get angry (a twitch of the eye, a frown… the words

that follow?) with the convenience of the circles of hell.
Neat and tidy as fire, which sweeps in here and takes us

all "out". We can hear heavy gunfire from the army's training
ground at Bindoon over 30ks away. Last week a fire

broke out where the shells fall, lighting up the bush
they haven't atomised. But the Easter lilies – the settlers'

flowers – are out in their pink rush, and the whole district
marks off the next stage of conquest. It's gradual, you see,

like comparing séga with maloya in La Réunion,
the feet on the ground dance moves of séga

and the beats of maloya crushed by the French in 1970,
both risen in Creole synthesis out of slavery, an anger

translated as exquisite action where a volcanic island
rises out of the deep ocean, prison and paradise.

JK

36.

For months, the small dog cowered at sudden movements –
the guilt in me covered my skin the way memory does:

the shame of my son, at eight, bowing quickly at my reach
to embrace, his eyes wide with knowing guile – my body

is ready for you, father. We called it spanking, and then repented;
there is shame in that, too. Still I grew up in Kingston

in that decade of blood, and still we pretended that the plague
or murders were news, though I knew from the magnet

that bloodletting was in the playfields, my body moving
away, while the hordes rushed towards the alarm and chaos,

the promise of slaughter; I knew that in my limbs was a strange
fear, something that smelt of cowardice, but that too is wrong –

the thing in us that makes us regard the violence of our bodies
as something ordinary. I have asked why it is I do not

carry in me the equation that allows me to see the grainy
images of the speed and simplicity of captured murder

without the swelling of my bowels opening up. That shit
I called fear, and sometimes the vanity of how much better

I am. Though, were I honest, I would say that perhaps
there has been a wayward mutation in me, or some kind

of defect making me turn away from the physics of killing;
this is the truth of it. *Wouldn't you kill for your family?*

he asks. Why must I contemplate such things? *Ahh, but you must,*
taste it first, know it well — the readiness is all. Another

of the ways I fail our race. What they tell me is that after
the first ritual, the rooster beheaded, the goat blooded,

the flagellation, the orgy of blood and water spilling
from his side, the purifying indulgence of the eating

of broken flesh and blood — verily, verily, the imagination
of the faithful — after this, the rest comes as easy

as shitting, pissing, and sleep. So they say, while skittish
me, I find myself on a street in Tunis thinking I have no stomach

for this, shameful me — all those bodies, all those useless
broken bodies. We all have it in us. Who? Who? Who said that?

KD

37.

To work with another – to collaborate – is a way for me… us…
to focus without being lost in who we are. But in hearing the pain

of another and all those focalised through their own lives, to wear
it through the figurative made literal on the field of the page –

the paddock just outside my door, the gunshots over the weekend
when I had to send our son indoors so shot didn't rain hot down

on him… a cultural shift, cultural difference, all fill the picture
with ourselves off-centre, moving through our own experiences

as observers and subjects at once. That's the failure of twentieth-
century-and-after explorations of subjectivity, those excuses

to look into the self without responsibility, a kind of displacement.
You don't allow me that, in the bloody streets of your shared history,

in who you are as poet and person. And male. We're blokes in this
together and carry the flexing of our gender, the lapses and trauma

we trail behind us like victory. I reconciled with my father fifteen
years ago. A massive, physically-driven man who was a footballer,

whose father would whip him with a strap and gained his respect
through doing so. He did the same with me, and my mother broke

the bond to reset things. An old man, my father is no longer aggressive –
he is witty and has broadened his notion of what it is to be "Australian".

He attended my brother's wedding to a Malaysian Muslim
wife and celebrated with genuine enthusiasm. Joy. His father

had been a state forester, a bushman, and my father was born
in the timber. Smart, he became a motor mechanic and worked

his way up. His sons were to be footballers but turned out poets
and artists and musos and shearers and drunkards and addicts

who wrecked masculinity. Out of the violence of the Irish
Great Famine, his great-grandfather and great-grandmother came –

"settlers", who switched languages and joined the occupation
of Noongah lands. The violence they would have seen –

the shifts that make Australia a parody of other New World nations,
and a corrosive shadow of the Old World that spawned it… Them.

So, I hear you, Kwame, and use every tool and trick (trickster?)
of dynamic equivalence I know. Our son, Tim, is homeschooled

because the bloodlust of this district is not confined to how
fathers and sons treat animals – in the schoolrooms, hate-crimes

are the lessons of the day. And on Saturday we drove to Mogumber
where the dead of Moore River Native Settlement are buried

beneath a thin layer of sand – killed by the State in so many
ways, the horror tactile and tangible, and no sleep will come of it.

JK

38.

Now is the season of side stitches, skin pinches and stinging eyes.
Half the night spent on a Tennessee bed too slack for my body
sent me to the stern floor where the chill and dander gather.

I become more man the less I know of my manhood,
the silences that seem far safer than the bombast
of knowing, and by man I mean male, not in the communal

way, but in the way a burden feels or how fat grows on me,
all this sullied flesh – a gift of unwanted bounty.
Here in Knoxville where our friends cook stewed fish

and salmon jolof rice, we visit the White Fort, a roomy homestead
with a kitchen where old Sally's bed sits in the corner
separated by the dog-shelter, an crude undercroft for cool refuge

for the dog days of summer – and there in that kitchen
she kept warm fires at night until the patriot was dead
and his will read – the field hands were freed, but precious Sally

was kept in the family – bequeathed to a nephew, a special
gift, with three hundred dollars for her upkeep and care;
these dubious legacies of goodhearted forefathers

(this is what they mean by a goodhearted man, yes?).
The stench never leaves at each turn in the genteel south,
though waiting in the still blizzarding Midwest is the erasure

of self, the polite disappearance before the ragweed
and pollen, the aches, pricks and terrible cramps.
Lorna and I are flying back to the spring rains,

and gentle is the air between us, as if the looming
fear of rupture has passed now. Laugh enough,
push out that air held long with anxiety, let the body

shake, force the eyes to water, and soon the orgasmic
lamentations of laughter released become the purifying
of the false heart, and the new true face will glow,

amazed at the healing of choice. I have tried this
while standing in the swamp of history – are these daguerreotypes
of field hands and kitchen slaves the revenant of

my people? I know them by the way their faces look
like my half awake Fanti family, uncombed hair and dream-
slung eyes – this is the haunting of tribal memory.

Knoxville, Tennessee.

KD

39.

Where we come from is bound
by those we live with? Your self
fused with Lorna's history, mine
with Tracy's. What do they think
of this? We probably know. We
could ask. We do in so many ways.

Once... once... when things weren't
as they are now, when things weren't
good... my addictions raging and my
control entirely gone: smashed windows,
bad scores that left me ill, crashed
out in limestone caves where
the whalers came in under the hell-
hole Roundhouse gaol, and death
was geometric, perverse as sailing
south to swing back to the trade routes.

Once... once... I left the wrecks
I had made, the house I had undone,
and journeyed to the Cocos Keeling Islands
to cut myself off from "the scene", only
to fall into the whisky trap of West Island,
where the world's criminals hid on a few
kilometres of land, looking searchingly
across the lagoon to the Home Islanders,
the Cocos Malays whose heritage
was indentured labour, the search
for freedom and their own way.

As a cyclone edged the islands
we bunkered down in the communal
centre (the administrators played Brandon
Lee's unfinished movie, *The Crow*)

and I went into delirium tremens.
When the all-clear was given,
the island doctor whisked me away
into a hospital bed and I watched
mainland spiders crawl up island walls.
The humidity melted my passport
in this Australian Territory.

In animist beliefs touching Islam,
I watched spirits moving through
coconut palms, scattering palm hearts
onto the coral sand. I processed
Charles Darwin and swore sobriety
if I could make it home. Arrested
on Christmas Island (taken off
the plane), I convinced the Feds
I would reform... then Tracy
found me (literally) at a motel
back in the city, Perth,
where I was born.

It was about my mistrust, the failure
of masculinity. An island affair. A loss
of focus, hallucinations of where I was
and where I had been. I flew to London
in the name of experimental poetry
and fell in with the Yardies – brothers
who took me in then shocked me
for a final time. Been "straight"
ever since. And with Tracy.

JK

40.

Bald now, the blood slippery where the nicks are –
all smooth, Akua says, her warm palms resting long
on the skull. Like this, I feel fatter still, and such

confessions pretend to be the alarm, but are merely
evidence of a man's lack of industry. In Lincoln,
before the greening of trees, this dry time of sharp

chill and brown brittleness is, despite the sunlight,
something morose, the mood of a ritual drive
through the emptying town to the stolid mute brown

box of a building whose basement is the sterile
dialysis center, or maybe where people nod off
on the chemo drip, in the humming fluorescent light;

to die like this is to die in late winter when even
the hope of warmth has grown tiresome. To think
I let my body's thickening consume me thus –

I eat tangerines by the bag, pegging, splitting,
pegging, splitting, counting the hours before
dusk, the days without sweat, the days ahead.

Yes, I've shaved my head again, and the constant pain
from the nicks are never enough to complain of,
never the stuff of great dramas. I betrayed

in the most mundane ways, and still have not
learned the language to turn it all into verse;
it lacks the neat catastrophes of tragedy,

and how easy it is, even after these monkish
years of penitence, to rehearse it all as farce.
Nicks, scratches, scattered stubble, ingrown hairs,

returning to their roots: these are the wearisome
metaphors – the truth is something else. I made
a deal: twenty years, to restore the years the canker

worms have eaten. Five years in, the edges
of the field are greening. It is something. We rebuild
in increments, one ordinary day at a time.

KD

41.

Yes, we do piece it together, draw the edges
to the centre, folding ourselves in on ourselves.
A shot just fired – ricochet through the valley –
that double percussion, false prophet breaking
of barriers to end the life of… fox, corella, cat,
roo… person? A weird suction, asphyxiating
annihilation of air.
                    It's hard to refocus, recall
what I was going to say while the hunter
moves through the reserve, his in-your-face
version of outdoorsmanship we all have to live
with and die for. A proclamation of the local.
The evening light is nipped
                         bronze and tempered blue,
the quasi-mystical creatures of night
are poking heads out and withdrawing
back into their sleeps.
                    I find it astonishing
that when I was a kid I traipsed around Wheatlands,
breaking the gnat-filled webs networking
saltbush and marsh grass into the crystalline
world of "the salt", rifle slung over my shoulder
and cartridge belt slung low on khaki –
                              in my
isolation making myself invulnerable,
                              re-enacting
and recreating self, face burning, the twin
peaks of Keats and Asimov in my pockets,
explorer colonist… but one cast out into
the wastes for being "weird".
                    Where was I?
And here, wondering if a stray bullet
might take one of us out; through the trees
no one is to be seen and the sun has almost gone.

JK

42.

Tonight the Okee Dokee brothers will sing adventure songs
in the granite-block Lied Center. Tomorrow, those prancing
Ailey Negroes with all their circumstance will leap
across the stage. Outside, the prairie grass multiplies
and a sharp wind drudges up history. Oh for history's
sake, the confederates are back in the great plains museum,
with the woven textiles and the overdue confession
that northerners enjoyed the softness of cotton
and the pulped currency that build a nation with slaves.
Tonight a Filipino American will stand before that flag
and rant post-colonial verse while the news travels.

As children, we were not starving, but cameras might have lied
convincingly. We were a marauding horde, a pack
roaming the Legon campus, scooping tadpoles, picking yoyis,
making up myths of the dark, long-limbed aunty and her gin
and cigarettes and kenke and fish and her Jackie O shades,
with her husband, the sandals-wearing, black-slacks-and-a-pipe
writer to think the classicist's thoughts, the species-destroying
beasts that we had invented, and were hungry
enough, after ripe mangoes had edged our teeth,
to roam the halls of residence, enter the dining room
and scrounge on the plates of leftover sausages
and bacon before the howl of the porter, before we went
sprinting into the open lawn and running out of shame,
for shame. How Mama found out remains myth,
how she beat us, legend, how we remember,
well art or the minstrelsy of okie dokey and guffawing
lies of our broughtupsy. Here is why I wear large clothes
to lose weight, and frump around swallowed by fabric;
we make our art, to put a fine point to it, to dance
loosely about us, and let them guess, let them guess.

KD

43.

Graves disease – hyperthyroidism – has left me
so "rapid" that the weight falls away and I walk
thin between the trees. A strange shedding of experience,
step by step, hastening towards a vanishing point.

Each excursion we make takes me back through
the bushlands of my childhood where my father
showed me the stuff he was made of, where my mother
was adventurous, but part of a poem of her own making.

It was never going to work. The threads of family
and cultures sidestepping to make common ground,
to work long and short-term memory-loss as stones
across the once clear-flowing creek, to paraphrase

the vanishing species with cats' eyes silver nitrate
through night stretched to breaking point. Mum
on the piano, a copy of Xenophon's *Anabasis*
open on the upright's top as if ready for Alexander

to pick up, glance at, take notice. But then, gathered
at the farm like a last supper, the Big Bible with
its carved cover, its marker on Isaiah, Chapter 9, 2:
"The people that walked in darkness have seen

a great light: they that dwell in the land of the shadow
of death, upon them hath the light shined…" as the fruits
of the harvest shone in the silos and I plotted with my
cousins how to turn the farm into an American

Wild West scenario, the marks of the people
whose land it was gnawing away at the feet
of the table, the foundations of the house,
the salt scalds. And today… and always today…

I take your poem, Kwame, in my head out onto
the land, out on yet another of my endless walks,
out into the possum country of Goomalling, out
to Oak Park where sheoaks on the edge

of the dead dry lake sing in the breeze,
the voices of ancestors who are not mine,
and though I can hear them I don't know
what they say, and the lake itself punctured

with thousands of dead eucalypts, pins and insects
in the killing jar of survey and farm, of wheatbelt.
And with Tim and Tracy a short way behind – Tim
studying lichen on granite – I happen on a couple making

love, or more to the point, fucking plein air, out in the open,
public sex in remnant bushland, the woman's thighs and buttocks
stretch open, exposed, the man beneath her, transfixed
as she lifts and falls on his penis. Below the sheoaks,

on the edge of the dead lake. I call out, Hoy! Enough!
A child is just behind me. And she breaks away and with
a swift motion places him under his shirt and covers
herself. It's deft. He grumbles, Sorry, we didn't know

anyone else was around, and she looks troubled. Don't worry
I say, it's just that you can't have a kid stumble
across something like… this. Tracy tells me later
that as she walked past she didn't look at him,

but caught her eye and smiled to show no harm,
doesn't matter. Tim, leaping from the lichen
springs after us and says, What's the matter?
What were they doing? Why did Dad yell out?

We tell him they were just going to the toilet.
Oh, he says, embarrassed, and takes off down
the track to study some animal prints in the sand.
All these writings-out. These rewritings. The marathons

through the discontinuous narrative, the alien familiar.
Tim has the angst of belonging and not, of wanting
land returned. Born in Ohio, raised in the Cambridge
fens and on the redstone of West Cork, at home

in the Western Australian wheatbelt, on Noongah
boodja. He sees a lot, but fortunately not everything.
There are some things we cannot fully explain,
or not yet. And what he unravels in his telling

later, much later, will leave out what affected us,
but be far more detailed for it, his eye tracking what we miss.
I am thin with Graves and worry and an odd exuberance.
All of it, all of it the lyric and its utter, utter trashing.

JK

44.

The father said it was a red floral dress
with white trims – flowers, too – and there is
a flat tone of resignation, as if this is how
each day unfolds. But what we cannot hear
is the deepest silence of the night as he stretches
out, trying to muster something he can only
call hatred – a violent thing to turn the dull
sun-blasted empty street of his insides
into meaning. How do you avenge a daughter's
murder against the incomprehensible. The Nairobi
churches will pray, sing hymns, offer a hand
for healing. I have sweated like this before,
and I have never known how to move my body,
how to make my face, how to conjure
the tragedy of loss, except as a selfish lament,
rehearsing how I have failed them, how I can
carry the burden of all tragedies. John, you
must know this space between the feeling
and the words we put here; we have mastered
the art of charting a myth of pain or laughter,
and should I not feel shame to admit that I have
never wept while writing a poem, never
stood on a hill staring at my village of a life
and wept as a faithful romantic for my craft?
A poet said today that between six and twenty-
six, he wanted to die, and poetry gave him
a reason to live; and I thought that he, that
lapsed holy ghost man, carrying in his flesh
the betrayals of the pulpit, is better than me,
more righteous a poet, or maybe a charlatan,
for I have never been able to say how poetry
saved my life. I can't even conjure a story
of this. I have almost died before. A car, the blood,
the broken bones, and some people saved

my life, and none were poets. Once I wanted
to cut away poetry like one cuts away
a hand that offends or an eye that betrays
with what it hungers to see and see and see,
or even a tongue, reptilian and pink muscle,
for the seductions I have unfurled with it;
and then the craft was an enemy to my body,
I thought, a contagion on me because
of how easily I pulled out those images,
how I could transport the unsuspecting
into their own perdition. It was a vanity,
that thought, and died quite quickly. Things
die. The prairie grasses, pulled cleanly from
the Sandhills, roots and all, will stretch fifteen feet
if pinned like a grand insect against a wall,
and that, too, is a kind of art – what it means
to have a monstrosity of roots hungry for
water, having to go deeper and deeper, having
to clutch stone and soil against the prairie winds
rushing over this bone-heavy land where things
die, quickly rot, the scent of decay vanishing
in days, leaving the dry taste of salt in the air.
I confess a lie here – this is a pretence, this bold
denial of the poem's healing – the truth is
more embarrassing. I confess that my life
is preserved by the trivial pleasures, the small
elations of what a mind can conjure, the music
it makes, these thin tendrils, like hair follicles
growing longer and longer, until they tangle
themselves into the weight of my comfort;
this is how I weather the storm, how the making
of things may fill that bleak night of lament,
the daughter's mouth reaching for mercy
before the violent silence that mauls her.

KD

45.

Each letter a tomb,
each word a cemetery –

what can we write
but memorials,

tributes, eulogies?
Haunting repetition.

Today, in Australia
the far right marched,

countered by those
of the Socialist Alliance.

The "Reclaim Australia"
patriots shouted "Aussie

Aussie Oi Oi Oi!" –
parochial death chant

hoping their fast bowlers
will take off someone's

head. It happened this year;
someone died. It was no

enemy as there's no enemy
at their doorsteps, but

they are conjuring demons,
wrapping themselves

in the flag: a Union Jack
with smattering of stars:

the Southern Cross.
It's the cross of their Crusades,

where white warriors
riding scramble bikes

out of the deserts
where pastoralist heroes

perished breaking the back
of an ancient country.

They are roused
by beheadings,

the anguish and pain,
the idea of an enemy.

They are roused
from their beers,

their hatreds – their
"way of life." Some

wear portraits
of the bushranger

Ned Kelly on their
t-shirts, his murderous

rampage their act of resistance –
their calling to account.

They claim "Halal
funds terrorism".

They claim "our
way of life".

Out of a tragedy-
in-the-making, patterns

of words emerge – memorials,
tributes, eulogies

hopefully before their time,
hopefully not needed.

JK

46.

You will know your heart by your allies, they say,
and at FAME Studios Alabama, Pickett sang, "Hey Jew",
and meant it as a kind of love song from a tough,
gunslinger city black man to the myth of his destruction –

"Hey, Jew, don't be afraid", to horns and the bass
of white men funking up the joint for Aretha
and all those collard-juice-sopping soulsters
looking to make their bodies a howl of redemption,

their voices like a streak of blood on the lintels.
In sixty-nine, in a DC church basement, a fist is raised while
the remembrance of deserts, parting seas, bushes
burning is turned into revolution; this revolutionary's

Seder: *What is God all burnt up about, pilgrim?*
What is the news today, sore-foot traveller? Why are you
still weeping on, sweet mother; has it not been a year
since y'all laid Martin's bones to rest; why all this burning?

I am not bright enough to drag these musics
together – I am simply standing at the edge of water,
or the prairie, or the vantage point where old Frost
stood, (weary now of people, finding his communion

among the lolling junipers, he of the fickle way,
coming and going as it suits him, no convictions
but sardonic neutrality) and pick up these musics
in the air like Peter Tosh, waving his antennae

and finding curiously, only the harmattan dust
and the scriptures against Babylon swirling over Kingston,
there at the edge of that sea. John, I was explaining
our exchange to, Ron, a young poet, and saw his envy,

and I said it was an unlikely grace with all the noises
in my head: the Test of nineteen seventy-five, with Lillee
and Thomo, and poor tiny Kallicharan with his busted
pants, hooking, hooking, hooking away; his face

wide open to take the blows – every survival a miracle,
and the cocky Aussie lips moving, the ironic grins, the strut
at the taste of blood – to think that this is what
they taught us, how to draw blood and keep it bleeding;

but that was cricket, and there were rules, and pads,
and this new thing is far less forgiving in its mercilessness –
we are laid open, forced to answer the whisperings inside of us,
the nagging doubts of language. I told him I am writing

elegies, a suite of elegies to what is to come, and the news
feeds us so many dead, and we must call it the news,
for if we stop calling it the news, then our clothes
will carry the pungent scent of mourners, the stale

muggy oppression of a home where the living
are trying to make something holy of their sorrow;
and if it is not news, we will break, and if not poems,
we will break. Here is the pall of helplessness

that covers over me when I read "Oi, oi, oi!". Ushered
out to the middle, the machinery of the bowling team
is in their easy flex and languid muscularity – the bowler
has the eyes of a man who will swing a machete

with efficiency, then gulp water for the thirst – and in this
I am alone, waiting, bat tapping, and the sound of his feet
thumping, and the soft chuckling warnings from slip,
Cut im t'roat, Percy, cut him t'roat. It is short, sharp,

then winding of pain, my arms and legs disowning me;
around me giggles, offers of aid, feigned concern,
the bowler staring at me as if willing me to fall,
so I do, to my knees, and I understand the way pain

has no home – it spreads like shame over everything.
This is the moment, still alone, my team-mate avoiding
my eyes at the other end – he too has fled – and the umpire's
bald head shaking. Out here I know that there are five

more balls to go, and I cannot hit back, I cannot run.
I have no answer to the imperious power over me.
And this is the singular moment that has repeated itself
again and again, not with bat and ball, but with the rituals

of living in this heavy world – the helplessness
of helplessness, and Baldwin called it shame,
and I thank him for it; and I thank you for making me
find these musics I have harboured, the ones that turn

companion in an alien land – the shadowy body,
a brown hooded form walking ahead; a presence
that always belongs, that infects even the most hostile
of worlds with my meaning – envy this, Ron, only this.

KD

47.

Rouse up in wake, wrestle the plough,
take no twee as polite emollient, task as Dr Know
shreds guitar in Bad Brains' "House of Suffering",
mirror fodder while on the way to overdose house,
arm slammed in door and DOA to rise and shine
with adrenaline, full quota hallelujahs of cool – old school;
taste a shutdoor policy, tunnelled through to ride ride
no envy to idiom loss a fuzzbox no pedestrian
wanderings collating postcards and souvenirs,
photodeath to stare into and trace the shady
images of palimpsest – such neglected layers
shrieking to get out – stomp and shout origins
to be heard above the palm tree or eucalypt
din, watching flame embrace the tree, full tree
out of ya tree of life tree of snake limbs
hydra narratives overload with throaty effusions –
but goddamn! it doesn't hurt to be polite,
and you can take me anywhere with
Andy Warhol hair, this classical rendition
of underworld juju polyphony where stress
takes a bow, all tribes come home to roost.

JK

48.

These mornings I wake with the bone-ache
of an athlete, but it is merely age
and the haunting of novelists – those long-winded
tellers of tale. At night I wrestle angels and lose.
I wake first in gloom, then wait for light.

I am stammering – it's not the words,
it's the music that eludes me;
language comes from attitude,
a kind of landscape, and here
there are no mountains, no sea.

The village built on the city's waste
still smoulders on the edge of the sea,
and in the air the ash of lived lives
consumed by the flame lingers;
I have not been in Kingston for months.

That year a negro appeared unto Natasha
Rostova as if in a dream, and she held it
with her brother, Petya, to be the secret
pathology of adults, how they lied
and said there were no negroes in Russia.

Upstairs in the deepest valley of Legon
I stay awake for the drumming
and I know a knife is healing a child,
the poor dumb rooster giving all,
and the heart finds the pulse.

Now the birdcalls are colonizing the air.
Why is it that some moonless mornings
are brighter before sunrise than others –
cloudless, too? I make a mystery
of ordinary things – Lorna does not respond.

So I collect delights: the girl laughing like my daughter –
I can't believe I cussed in front of him! –
on a grey brisk Nebraska morning, the shared
smile, the intimacy of mild transgressions,
my too short trouser legs in the passing window.

And lunch at last with the bearded boy
saying, *I bought your book in the bookstore,*
good stuff dude, good stuff! And how we laugh
with our soft bellies and caps, before the gloom
of our elegies, John, our necessary elegies.

KD

49.

This exorcism? An exoneration of impact;
the space we occupy? Last night I had a flying
dream – I'd pull on a pair of old jeans with holes
at the knees and I'd fly, fly like I did in the old days.
Jeans off and I'd be grounded, landlocked. Another
dream saw me driving a car along the coast – maybe
the west side of the Mizen Head peninsula, front
wheels pulling me onto wave-buffed but still sharp
rocks. That was the sense of it. Not much of a narrative.

Lots of stuff is coming out in the wash. A lot of churning
and grinding in the breakers. Full sets of seven. My brother
surfs a place called Hell's Gates off Geraldton where
a tiger shark undershadows his movements waiting
for the next bone-crunching wave. So far, it has only
snacked on the snippets of soul that have broken off
as each ride ends or he is wiped out. He has plenty
of soul to spare but being sinewy and tough – a shearer –
there's not a lot of fat for the shark to chew over.

In our "bad old days" he looked after me more
than I looked after him. He's almost three years
younger, but he was more level-headed when
the crunch came – getting me out before the neo-Nazi
gang attacked the house, or steering me away
from a bad scene, a bad scene he would fall
into once I'd vanished. Now, sober, we are
close at a distance. But we always know,
we always know. We listen out for birds

at evening, reconfiguring their messages
wherever they call from, wherever we are.

JK

50.

My bones have grown used to this standing,
this upright posture; the rituals of rising, unfolding,
and then lowering have grown wearisome, painful.
So I loiter in the back of halls, trying to disappear;
it is how I stay awake through the drone of language.

Tomorrow, fifteen thousand people will circle
each other, eyes darting around for the assurance
of our importance, being recognized; so much
desperation in one place, as if this is art. Mostly
it is fifteen thousand people being almost famous.

It is telling that I have lost the genius for fantasies –
not the imagined pleasures, those entrances and exits
of bodies willing to do my bidding, nothing so tedious –
no, the dream of a cottage, perhaps, near the sea,
with the comfort of green vegetables and fish.

This is how it starts, and then the noise of logistics
crowds in, the deadlines nagging, the unfinished
letters, the weight of idleness; I envy monks,
the ones who say nothing and walk in gardens
smelling of oranges, and talk to God who, I am told,

is happily profound even on bad days; then there are
the birds, dotting the grey sky, the stark lines of leafless
trees, the blasted heath – that kind of thing – and stones,
limestone statues outside caves, picking wild fruit.
Shall I say none of this is appealing, really, just the idea of it.

My brother – one of them – comes to me in waves
of crisis, and this is the guilty value of migration – the buffer
it makes between the annoying rituals of empathy,
the guilt for anger at the helpless, and all of this –
coffee in the morning, watching the sun's nonchalance.

Here is where the road changes into a dirt track,
here is where we ask about the language we speak,
here is where the meaning of things unsettles us,
for when we arrive at the road's end, we are sweating
and this is all we have to show for it.

Last night, during the most manipulative of films,
I wept for a woman who, after failing at everything,
stood on stage clumsily, but sang elegantly, and I thought,
well this makes it all worth it – if we can sing, or make
others weep, or conjure the coast with its sharp rocks,

and a man's vulnerable body balancing on a board,
hurtling towards the sand – no matter the context –
for me, it is five in the morning, and my brother, to beat
back demons, has ran five miles on the peninsula,
where a woman, wrapped against the early chill,

peels golden ribbons of orange skin, exposing the sharp
white to the pink light, cuts the top off, so this brightness
of juice gleams, and hands it to him. She will tell him
her secrets, and he will tell her his secrets, and they will suck
oranges, and stare into the sea. It stops there, before

the growing traffic, the noise in his head reminding him
of what is to come, before she thinks of who will come
to buy fruit, before it is all shattered – this reverie – there is
the sense of it, exactly what happens with these songs –
they become about what we want, what we imagine we want.

They are not what is – my brother never runs, and if he does
it ends badly, a circling around memory, some dizziness
before they find him blowing in the wind. And I never run.
These bones, these smoothed down bones; and, yes,
tomorrow, I join the limping convocation of poets.

KD

51.

I have become more "antisocial" with the years –
or maybe, truth be told, more eremitic, more

contained wherever I am. Inland, it's the wind
sweeping in and blocking everything else out,

or by the coast, the working of waves on rock.
My days of being on the road – month on month –

have gone, but if a financial crisis threatened
I would probably go back to the stage – small

crowds listening to snatches from the West
Australian wheatbelt, an alien world where

I am merely an impediment to the regime
of monoculture and the liberty of unimpeded

prospects, the ongoing reinvention of colonial
histories, the ley lines of markets and profit,

that dreamed-of end result of familial
cultural revolutions increasingly occupied

by multinational companies, or privateers.
And so many roads that switch from macadam

to gravel, or even the loop we live on that would close
us in should fire sweep in, a letter C of doom, script

of foreclosure. We too watched a film last night,
Mon Oncle d'Amérique by Alain Resnais

wherein neurosurgeon Henri Laborit, he of soldiers
and dopamine, enacted his philosophies on the audience

and rats – electric shocks – response… satire
on us, of us, with us as victims of evolution

that Resnais played out to the hilt, sad perverse
absurdism; animal cruelty ruined it for us, the rats.

JK

52.

I am a hopeless gardener, but I have come to enjoy
these metaphors, these elaborate rituals of carving

our cicatrices of self – Herbert, Milton, and Dryden.
A gentle old Englishman in the colonies

taught us these rebels against chaos, the secret
hunger of those colonisers with their caked powder

skins and such foul odours, the facade of grace,
and their verses taming the roguish misbehaviour

of the woods with the ordering of gardens, colonies of gardens.
I have always known the uncurling of tender green shoots

from seeds in cotton balls to be miraculous, and such
miracles of things surviving in my care to be part of my ill luck.

They die. I am the labourer, the digger of holes,
I obey her rules and stand witness to her holy hands

making these beautiful children into living humans
who sprout thoughts, surprising with their foliage.

Who knew we could make such colour? I know nothing
of weeds and insects, all I know is that I collect

any orphan sprout or seed I find, and keep things
musky and damp enough for rot that something might root

such delightful gifts – call it junk – but see how they grow.
Here is the catalogue of unearned delights:

Alvin Ailey Dance Theatre, "Lift"

...and then they gather in the light's pooling,
an oil canvas in motion, their bodies
caramel, ebony, tan, purple, begin that slow
bounce, gentle, gentle, lifting till their heads
are raised up, up, up as one.
This weapon of our health, the impossible
machinery of such well-tutored bodies;

a kind of delight in the body's dialect,
a laughter of movement, the one thing
certain they can do, even while the mundane
disasters of their lives close in on them;
this one thing they can do again and again,
turning as one machine in the fading light,
there, lift, lift, lift, lift, lift, lift, lift!

Alvin Ailey Dance Theatre, "Four Corners"

...there is the dust, and then the sun arrives,
we shade our eyes with the soft filter of scarves
and the voice of a woman with the sweet of dates
and the promise of rain gathers about us,

and, and, and the korah's tongue licks
the pimpling of sweat, the gourd echoes our hearts
and below it all is the ground thump,
the hiccup of stop time. Watch them come,

their bodies set low but eyes alert, syvah, syvah, syvah,
dinki mini, brukkins, bogle, making their waists
turn, and the right foot grows numb, a kind of
crippled grace so fluid, so easy the way

we fall into the Africa of it, the caught breath
of it. Tonight, I remember how dance
defies all our words; we watch the miracle
of bodies floating across the stage – stop, go, stop go...

Minneapolis/ St. Paul

...these streets have the grey drabness of a city
scrubbed of all colour by sleet and snow; the buildings,
practical bunkers against the ice, do not breathe,

and it is as if the sky's mute blandness dictates
the palette, so there is joy in the flare of white in the gloom
of a side café, the table a still life called "After Brunch",

the lip-stained cups, the flakes of golden crusts,
the smear of jelly, the deep yellow patina of a broken yolk,
the crumbled napkin sheltering the winking silver

of the cutlery scattered around the tablecloth.
I stop to watch as if caught in the hidden narrative
of a morning's ritual; I can fill these grey mornings

with the hypnotic incantation of a simple song:
blueberry jam and runny eggs; this is how we said goodbye,
this is how we said goodbye, this is how we say goodbye...

KD

53.

How we choose what we bounce off, what we
connect through – dialogue with? – the pick-ups
and drop-offs, the arrivals and departures.
I know Minneapolis a little, and certainly
know the airport. I went there at a cold time.

I have been thinking about our constituent selves.
The mix that makes us all. My Londoner grandfather
who followed the "Pommy" cricket team with
vehemence, and as parochial with the Western
Australian team. Sailed here with his mother

and sister after the death of his father. I've told
this before, but I am telling in a different way
and it all adds up long after the players have gone.
My great grandmother played piano
for the silent movies, my grandfather

would later paint the advertising hoards,
posters. He was renowned for this in the
then small city of Perth. Or my grandmother,
his wife to be – eye on her for years – a goldfields
child whose father died of miner's disease,

dust on the lungs. We can all paint the weirdness
of these constituent selves. Should we? Which bits
hang over the ledge, fall to us by force of gravity,
persuasion of childhood wonder and bewilderment?
Here, an ordinary day…? Time spent with Tim

watching the second *Hobbit* movie, going out
and checking the fluid boundaries of the block after
rain, the lists of quotidian empathies. Food matters
here beyond the eating – a family of vegans –
so much has to be prepared from scratch,

and Tracy dedicates a lot of time to our diets:
the balances, the levels, the joy (& strain) of feeding
our flesh, our souls. Last night, sweet and sour rice
with garlic tofu, and tonight it's likely to be
seitan and roast vegetables because a deadly

summer has passed and the oven can run
without destroying us! We are isolated out here,
though there are distant neighbours who act
as if they are the only ones in the valley:
the boom boom boom of a mega stereo

playing dance music late into the night,
the tawny frogmouths linking the beats
with "mournful cry". Distance plays
havoc with our sense of connection,
our communications, but also intensifies

how we see and hear. To go out for a night
on Sunday we have to drive young Tim 90ks
to his grandmother's in the shadow of the sacred
mountain of Walwalinj, then drive another 100 plus ks
to the city, then another 100 plus ks home,

then repeat it the next day to collect him.
In between, wandoos hang on, haunt
and speak in peculiar tongues, growing out
at unpredictable angles above a certain height,
their trunks the embodiment of gravel

and ancient ecotones forced back
on their tails. The York gums with rough bark
and the jam tree with silver upsides when blown
by a southerly or easterly – flipside flipside –
and the drive that undoes the world.

JK

54.

He is fifty.

I had another thing to say,
then I saw what I have sought not to see,
and it stains my head's insides,
it interrupts the comforts of our bouncing,
leaves me with the endless song of grief.

He is a big man.

He wears black trousers.

He runs like someone who used to run.

He falls like an afterthought.

And dying looks so ordinary.

The man with the gun
shoots eight times,
says nothing,
shouts nothing.

Four in the back,
one through the ear.

He was fifty.
He was a big man.
He looked better in black.
His daughter picked out the blue shirt.

He ran like a man afraid
of the man who has said he was afraid.

He ran then fell like an afterthought.

The path is ordinary,
the South Carolina green is familiar;
you can feel the soft humidity in the air.

We die easily.

I once read Sir Walter Scott,
the stumbler, the limping one,
but he righted himself,
righted himself.
He did not fall on his face.

Two weeks ago, Nikky
wrote of the wisterias in bloom,
those purple clusters
of southern decorum,
of the season changing.
And when she said "wisteria",
I thought of the dogwoods,
their leprosy of stoic white
as if cast there to decorate
the new season. Those delights,

those were my rituals of Easter
in Carolina all those years.

It is true that what I see
behind that mute tableau,
the dumbshow of bodies
turning violent death
into something mundane,
is the purple pleasure
of wisteria, and a canopy
of dogwood leaves, snow white
in warm Charlestonian April.

I have stopped looking
at the crude obscenity of this,
so these colours, plus the green,
the black, the blue, the pink –
they stain the insides of my head.

We die like animals.
I can't continue tonight
as if this has not happened:

Me running.

Me stumbling.

I am fifty-three.

Perhaps I am wiser.

This is how we grieve strangers.
We grieve selfishly.
We grieve our fear.
We grieve ourselves.
We grieve our grief.
We grieve our grievances.
We grieve the things bigger than grief.
We grieve the way things are.
And maybe good Walter is lost in our grief,
and that, too, is what they stole from him.
They stole his grief.

KD

55.

I was about to add a coda
when yours came through, Kwame.
Far away, I register. The news
that is more than data. The loss
that is beyond implication
and is all implication, too.
How can...? How can the murdering
keep going on and on?

A great American poet
wrote to me yesterday and said
she can't take the news anymore –
she doesn't know where to turn.
The news that is us, that steps
in tune. The bullets cowboys
fire to make the nerd, the geek,
the fancy man jump hot-footed
in front of the frilled ladies
who want to be anywhere
but there, who have better
things to think about.

The coda I was going to send
was about my grandfather
winning a movie-poster
competition in the early 30s –
Alice in Wonderland –
with the newspaper
describing the colours
with relish in black & white.

He loved honky tonk.
He loved vaudeville.
He went to Russia

in the early 1970s
and wondered at the tomb
of Lenin – his embalmed lyrical-I.
He loved (and painted)
the Queen.
He went rabbit hunting
with my uncle – his son-in-law –
because that was bonding.
He was not a man
of war. Violence
was imaginary.

The coda I was going to send
also contained this news snippet
about an ancestor of mine,
unearthed by Tracy: "This is
Ned's nephew (*Bunbury Herald*, 7 July 1898)",
she says, then quotes: "From Karridale I learn
there are still a good many cases of fever.
It was also reported that young Thomas Kinsella
got his hand so badly crushed
by a corn crusher
that he had to have two
of his fingers amputated."
I got stuck on
                "crushed by a corn crusher"
and was going to write over:

"crushed by a corn crusher"
"crushed by a corn crusher"
"crushed by a corn crusher"
"crushed by a corn crusher"
"crushed by a corn crusher"
"crushed by a corn crusher"
"crushed by a corn crusher"...

in this family implosion of "early settlers"
and their progeny, in the deaths by fevers
and collateral damage of felling trees,
of the rural and the ecology
of occupation, the loss
of original language,
the writing over.

And then yours – I knew it, too.
I was born in February 1963 –
we are contemporaries
as death always is,
as each bullet fired
is the death of us all,
repeatedly. All the gun
manufacturers, the absolute
bloodiness of dissembling,
of "people kill people
guns don't kill people"
propaganda and its segue
into "race relations".

The misnomer's verse
feeds on pretending
it's not culpable.

Mea culpa
mea culpa
mea culpa
            "crushed by a corn crusher"
        "crushed by a corn crusher"
"crushed by a corn crusher"!

JK

56.

I think you will let me run; you will follow walking
at a brisk pace; soon I will be out of breath,
soon the pain in my ankle and knees will slow me,
soon there will be a fence between me and escape,
soon I will wonder about my heart, and you
who know my name, you who can see my body's distress
will chuckle softly, watching me sit, watching me saying,
Okay, okay, okay, you got me – and maybe we will
laugh, and you will say, *Man you need to lose some*.

And I will roll on my stomach and welcome the soft
damp cool of the grass, and you will then put on
the cuffs, and I will say, *Not so tight*, and you will say
How's that? and I will say, *Thanks,* and *Sorry, man,*
just got freaked by the taser, and you will say,
You know that was some stupid shit you pulled,
and I will say, *Yeah man, sorry,* and you will say
I could have shot you, and something about being
pissed off and all the damned paperwork,
and even though I'd want to, I won't say,
All this over a broken tail light? or,
You know you wrong to stop me, but I will say
I used to run better, and you will say, *Football?*
And I will say, *Yeah, we get fat after a while*,
and then the sirens of the back-up will fill the air,
and my heart will sink, but will still be beating
and that will be the end of the day, see?

How optimistic and forgiving of me to cast this all
in the future tense, as if I have some dream that someday
this is how a Blackman and a white cop will laugh
on a sunny Charleston afternoon; how forgiving
of me to avoid the judgement of the subjunctive,
of the abstracted hope of what might have been,

when we know that what has been
is an indictment of what might have been.
Old sinner man, where yuh gonna run to?
Downpressorman, where yuh gonna run to,
on that day, on that day, on that day?

So you know, I ran from you. I will run from you,
I would run from you because I grow stupid
when I am around you, and you might ask me
who *you* is and all I can say is *you* is not me,
which is never enough, but we are talking about
what has been or what is to come or what should have,
which is another way of saying we can't do a thing
about any of it, except to know you is not me.

KD

57.

This morning I saw a white-winged female fairy wren
on the top fencewire below the great York gum just
outside our front door. This is the second time in six
months that I've seen a bird we've never seen here
before. An affirmation? I latched onto it as such,
and its made a quiet spectacle out of the day.
Mainly, it's been chainsaws across the valley,
deteriorating with distance – seasonal shift
bringing teeth to dead or fallen or felled wood,
and stocks of firewood appearing along
outside walls. There's nothing like this in summer
when it's all cleared away – fuel to the conflagrations
that take bush, paddocks, sheds and houses. A spark
that demands more of its timeshare than is permissible.

This is not to distract from the seriousness of being
in the world, of the world, to crouch down low in the scrub
and hope it passes by. You can't do that here – a stray (or not so
stray) bullet will find you out. I have a cousin I spent much time
with as a child out on the farm, a cousin I loved and admired.
I still feel close to him though never connect, never spend time.
We've much in common as he plants trees and reclaims saline areas,
but in the end he still hunts and polishes his rifles with gun oil,
still reads myths of survival. When I turned against the gun
and all it stood for, we drifted… a breach… the breech. He also
has a wry sense of humour, loathes capitalism, though wouldn't
put it that way, in the house he built himself – power and light
he harnesses from the sun. He has a particular kind of knowing
but reserved smile. I miss it. But the paths are too divergent.

JK

58.

All who come into the world are called.
Open the curtain of spirit
       — Carolyn Forche

Today, John, my throat has the hint of irritation
as if my body expects to be laid low with fatigue
and done in by a wayward virus; I have been embracing
so many bodies. Once, I spoke of death
and realized, as the words left my body, that the sick
in my bones was a kind of death, an emptying.
I do not want the air around me troubled
by the words I speak, I do not want to speak
of the dead, to be the body of the dead;
I want the walls of bodies shifting about me
too long to leap, lift, leap and lift.

There is a quiet room far from the madding,
and I marvel at how gently my body falls
into a curve, takes to the cushion, closes in.
Inside my head there is the red dirt of some deep
warm land, the heavy green of oversized leaves,
and the sky is crowded with hurtling clouds
flimsy as a white silk kerchief. A rooster crows so that
I think of it as red, familiar as the soil's redness,
and Dellie's mother brings me a plate of fried fish,
sliced tomatoes, thickly buttered hardo bread,
and a glass of milk. She is waking me for daybreak,

To eat something, she says, *before you sleep again.*

She, too, is dead, and that I am dreaming her
is comforting. You see, I do escape to that womb
cottage, that soft-walled memory, when I tire
of the things I have been told to say, and from here

I can see my way to that walk through the dense
banana plot, out to the uneven paving of the road
beside the cane fields, and just when I feel
the slick of sweat under my arms, I can smell
the brine and musk of the sea long before
I hear it, long before I see it glimmering
after the bend in the road, but this dream
of the dead mother, the fish, the bread, the rooster,
the banana leaf, the cane trash, the glimmering
sea, this waking dream is the delight I long for.
This man has fallen in love with a dream.

Remembering Clonmel, St. Mary, Jamaica

KD

59.

Sometimes... often?... We don't
recognise ourselves in the descriptions:
birth records, marriage certificates (where and when,
where and when, where and when), comments
scribbled down by "observers" and officials
in government agencies and obtained
under the freedom of information
act... reviews... petty acts
of vengeance.

      When pundits
try to assimilate us into their
models of class, gender, sexuality,
when they ascribe cause and effect...

affect... ethnicity and heritage and tendencies
according to the names we are given
(or the names we have chosen)
...desire and hunger...
standard of education...
               without
a hint of the slippage that rolls
along the highway
we travel, but don't want
extended into wetlands
to boost industry and trade
via an expanded port facility...

            In fact,
because we find ourselves
on the highway, who is to say
we even want to be there? Who
is to say, who is to say
that we accept our being there
at all?

      Circumstantial evidence.

As if not voting is quietist
or an acquiescence to the state
rather than a resistance, a non-
participation.

These sinking ships!

These sinking ships on overexplored
and misunderstood
inland seas –
desiccated inland seas

where gypsum shines
like the stockmarket
but has nothing to do with it,
not even figuratively –

is profit
more to do with
pink bacterial deaths, more to do
with coastlines
and their lip-smacking tides
tasting of the siliciclastics
of sabkhas?
Depends on
the asking?
These
shifting tendencies, these
dislocations making
a hegemony of poets.

Surely we don't need ask "why do birds sing?"
as per Frankie Lymon and The Teenagers –

surely we know why
and don't need to prove it
to the woodwork?

JK

60.

The doctor tells me I will see.
Slipping these tiny plastic cups

to dance delicately on the coning
of my cornea, he promises light,

in waves of delight on all things.
We have done this before;

it has been four years,
and my eyes, with their

neatly stitched corneas,
have defied all miracles.

I am bored by promises;
it is as if I am being deprived

of an image – there is in my
family line a parade

of the aging blind;
and my mother in Kingston

has been hungering for light
for five years. *It is blackness*

now, she says. These days when
I call, she rehearses without irony

the litany of her body's betrayal,
beginning with the weight,

then the mystery of swirling
milk inside a glass of water,

the way all sound becomes
a pressure on her,

and I listen. This is the good
news from Kingston.

My father's father died in his
Lady Musgrave Road middle-

class bungalow in darkness,
the letters of his son

read to him by the older
son already in his cups

on that long steady march
to ruin. Are we damned Russians

in 1812, with an estate
of serfs catching the smell

of rebellion among the surly
French with their *Code Noir*

of indecency, and the rumours
of Toussaint and Dessalines,

and Napoleon, tiring
of those islands with their

funk of Josephine
and her coconut-oil hair,

and all that rebellion in her waist
longing for some other

triumph, something white,
colder, like Moscow

waiting like a frightened whore
for his arrival. Is that who

we are? The news from Jamaica
is not good; tonight, the daughter

of a dear friend drank herself
to boldness, tied a noose

around her neck and
is dead. My family is shaken.

The sedated mother is my sister's
best friend – they gather at night.

My mother, I know,
will pray into the soft

darkness, and we wonder
where our children are,

how dark it is on the roads,
what noises are being whispered.

KD

61.

My left eye almost went the way
of darkness last year, the jelly

torn away too rapidly, the burnt
spots edging my retina

dangerously close – perverse
circling of wagons. The news

that comes out of fading,
damaged sight is the gathering

of dull cloth, or as my besieged
Russian poet friend says

in response to my comments
on his latest book, "Dark should

contain hope, that is true…"
translating images from void.

Loss. He is sheltering in forest
emerging from snow drifts.

As we trace out our lists
of the dead in the poor light

we are stopped in our tracks
with another fallen, lost.

To Karen, who shed her
interior to a South American

dealer in body parts;
to Craig who made a sermon

as he marched into the Swan River;
to Niall who was taken by cancer,

rockstar of theory, distillation
of cool irony, fiercely loyal;

I live their deaths in my retina –
bright lights that shone

with different intensities,
at different points on the spectrum.

Walking Jam Tree Gully yesterday
I saw a great flock of pink & grey

galahs heading towards me
and I held opened arms

high in welcoming… but from over
the crest of the hill came the shotgun

blasts of a neighbour driving
them on and on, downing a couple,

blasts louder than the scrawled
calls of the galahs, blasts

that say there's no footing
on earth for the alive, the excited…

these are birds that can't land
anywhere. I watched them vanish

into the horizon, so much
closer than we realise,

taking our eyesight
for granted.

JK

62.

Somehow the buildings here are so angled
that the sunlight stops at the edge of the opposite wall,
a kind of stain, sharply marked down the flank
of pink. I imagine that four floors down there is
a courtyard of ferns, soggy peat, wide-leafed
shrubbery, and a colony of worms, bearing
on their cool skins the gleaming droplets
of moisture. No doubt what I imagine:
a soggy place walled off from all intruders
where two horny old folks, like rare
birds posing for adventurous watchers –
she in her loose slacks and silky tangerine
blouse, him with his cream slacks, light straw hat
and delicately embroidered cariba shirt –
make their rapid Spanish love – of grunts
barks and long drags of cigarettes. It's a secret
they have carried for decades, so that even
when his wife died and her husband left
for New York, as a final insult they pretended
secrecy – a kind of subterfuge that he says
is the only thing that makes him stand to,
that she says makes her think of loving him,
with his balding head and his liver spots.
To think that such elaborations of an epic,
like the detail of an out-of-control Baroque
painting, sinning in plain light, might vanish
were I to look down to see the white concrete
stretch of emptiness instead of tree tops,
a bench, shadows, and the music of two bodies
slowly coming together. This is San Juan
and I have willed myself to consume
nothing of its history and present, but instead
to stare across the shadowed gap between
my hotel room's window and the nondescript

grunt of the wall on the other side.
Yesterday, listening to Heaney at thirty-one,
his Irishness like pebbles in his mouth,
I thought how curiously neat were his poems,
how everything was a calculated metaphor
for this art – the plowing, the blacksmith,
the digging – and how indulgent it all seemed,
how mannered, and how like a man
reluctantly making a tradition, something
of an elaboration of himself; and then I thought
of how we lie when we are younger
so as to create these narratives of ourselves –
such harmless lies about how we make art
and what our art should be valued as.
A man spent so much time complaining
of how Frank McCourt made up all that squalor
and adventure of his Limerick life, and how
McCourt himself invented a squalid heroism
in petty thievery – the big black book of the debts
of the people which that Jewish moneylender
kept, which Frank tossed into the Shannon River.
So I think of the lies I have invented,
the fictions of my significance, the clear
logic and sequential elegance of my life,
from incident to incident, things I will never
correct, for if I even knew the truth, knew
the instant a memory became a story,
it has all left me now. Some things persist
despite all efforts to reshape them, like
my fear of blindness, like the weight
of blurriness every morning before I remember
to see where I am, like the persistent
off-white film at the edge of my right eye.
This fat man begins his morning light
as a fit footballer, then remembers
quickly, the strain of weight on the ankle,

and the blurring of all my body's lines;
this is a faulty metaphor for what we see
or do not see, what we invent or do not invent
and how, John, these letters we share
are charting each day our new inventions,
our new ways of seeing the world renewed.

KD

63.

We share a faded peripheral vision —
between us we have two good eyes
or are blind. Blind — always been
a word that's bothered me cast
as a moral pejorative, when lack
of vision can be stunning or devastating
insight. O Tiresias. Or do seers
always manipulate truth,
bereft of outline, the colouring in?
The snakes are going to sleep here
as the Autumn sets in.
                              Ouroboros.
I have been embroiled in my own
failure to recollect intention — not so
much dropouts in memory, though
they too are an essential part of the picture,
but epiphanies of linguistic loss,
the decay of puns and slippages: an
awareness that "experimental" has an in-
built atrophy, that an effort to step out
means there'll never been perfect
measurement: the length of wood
or metal roughly a yard or metre
will be found out over mile or kilometre,
so far out it might mean disaster.
We so often forget our secret
purpose of back then.
                              Ouroboros.

The avant-garde is in constant need
of resuscitation, where even
pronouns are desirably
unstable, but leave the future
bereft and even amused

out our sincerity,
our commitment to change,
to shaking it up.

                  I wonder
if I ever really had a sense
of the sacred? I wonder
if I ever respected syntax
(locked into it as I now am)?

In my days of addiction I relied
on moneylenders (Cash Converters),
and I am still grateful that they
turned a blind eye, that one gave me
two-hundred and fifty dollars
for the *Complete Oxford Dictionary*
that came in a box in two volumes
with a strong magnifying glass;
that the broker lamented
how low I'd gone… saying
that if I never came to collect
he'd keep it for his kids.

I never did. The money
got me out of a debt
over which I would have
lost my kneecaps. I was
running in circles
without finding
where I'd left off.
                  Ouroboras.
My nickname at school
was Dictionary – a mantra
of hate, barely
innovative. *Ouroboras.*

JK

64.

The poets from that island loiter on the beach,
carrion-hungry, making jokes salty as the sea
about the stubborn maestro who they know
has not decided whether it is shame or fear
that he disguises as love of them, of this island,
but it is one they know, for the love is an affectation,
the desperate performance of a manic actor
building each day the myth of his humanity
by forgetting all his dusty yesterdays. *The more
I forget, the better a human being I become,* he chuckles.

And he has cast in slanting hexameters, repeated
the metaphors of sea and darting swift until he too
has forgotten where the art overtook his nagging
embarrassment. Once he wrote of an insouciant woman
kissing her teeth and spitting her distaste for him
and how he wept for her: *My island, my people!*
His foreign friends have made a ritual of returning; it is their reward,
their repeating premature *dead lef'* wake
and sort of rehearsal of mourning each anniversary
for their sycophantic bowing and scraping.
They gather about him to be bullied, insulted,
while they draft small unfinished elegies for him
waiting for his bullying laughter to be silenced for good.

But the local poets hobble on the edge of the yard
where the grass ends and the sea begins, and he asks
his now war-hardened but faithful Nordic caretaker,
*They still out there? They still out there? But what the arse
they wanting from me? It's like they trying to shame
me into pouring rancid coconut oil on one of their heads,
like they think just because I keep warding off
death by welcoming it as prophecy, that I ready
to step aside for one of them, and who are they anyway,
but some stuttering versifiers, earnest pretenders.*

Here we see how history is translated into fairy tales.
Literatures demand that we move towards history;
this memory you see triggers other histories.
The poet once wore powder to hide his black face,
such self-negation in an artist will elevate his art,
turn the most ordinary line into a gangrenous wound,
a quality of green that startles us: *I have spawned*
a tribe of mimics. They bring their fire-etched slabs
of driftwood and say, see, maestro, look how well I've done.
My trembling hand must anoint with a twisted glee;
they are mastering my ugliness. I feel I am in a hall of distorted
mirrors, and I remain the grudging sun.

The maestro laments, rheumy eyed, and they commiserate,
in the shadow of coconut fronds. But here is what I say:
All great lives offer a map of aging, how to carry their weight
of failure that is the lurking shadow over all triumphs,
how to wake daily looking to step away from the yawning
grave of content, and just keep walking to the next
isolated beach, a kind of discovery of the art of discovery
again and again, like you are the only one who can do this;
how to be that soul, alone in the world, and still longing
to be ready to sit on the grass one noonday, and let
your legs hang over the edge, and your peace come
over you, while those people walking towards you
through the coconut grove with all the accoutrements
for shrine building, with fire, rum and water, with song;
how to say welcome to this flock of lament and praise,
with grace or something more satisfying, contentment?

KD

65.

When you mentioned you were on an island
I thought of the island of granite we visited
over the weekend. A regular haunt. And I
configured it as retrieval and reception,
and typed "Death of Spotted Jezebels
Over an Outcrop of the Yilgarn Craton":

The killing jar summer is over
and late heat working the granite outcrop
at Gathercole fuses falling butterflies
to its contraindicative glint – sharp & muted –
water uneasy and rapidly evaporating from gnammas,
that rain reboot of last week. They're probably
spotted jezebels, these butterflies,
flying against their own weight and shape,
spent now and losing aviatronics, eggs laid
and passing into the particle world, coming to their ends
among the exfoliations and breakdowns of boulders –
fractured eggs and Russian dolls scattered and left ruined
after the break-up of the estate – an analogy entangled
with the island ("oasis") nature of conservation
in the blanks of farming. After all, as the jezebels
fall and die before us, tattered beauties,
where are we to go with our human concerns
with gender and tyranny, laws of behaviour, the way
we apply names to distance or remake or assert
ourselves? A sign spiked into a crack in the outcrop
says it's like "elephant skin" in its breaking down,
and as we wander, weighed down by flies –
flies shuttering photographs as doppelgängers
and facts – we risk, we are enamoured
of the weirdness, the grotesque, the fabulous.
But mammal and reptile scats, tracks
in traps of sand accumulated in hollows

show a pragmatism of presence – roos,
rock dragons – that shadows artistry,
a visual hunger, a lust for rendering
into display. It is not a gallery,
and as jezebels fall in their hundreds,
we step around their beautiful deaths, so caught-
up in our own impressions, what we will take away
and what will take us along the narrative tongues of axons,
to be taken up by the listening leaves of dendrites,
this array of synaptic activity on an outcrop
of the Yilgarn Craton, where neurones
we are losing – a withering supply –
help us forget what forces are at work.

JK

66.

There is a world of crisp air and a kind
of pickled snobbishness that comes

with these spired cities and villages
of the northeast – a chain of settlements

tidy as the ordering of the earth's
chaos – a life that can make a black man

from a small fist of an island say, *I am falling
in love with America*, for him then to lament

the departure of the muse, as if she makes her
appearances in Greyhound buses and post

offices. I am still learning to chart this landscape,
and every time I feel settled, she vomits me up,

beaching me on rocks and sand, tells me
I am too much for a sensitive stomach.

In the South, the dead things reek in the heat,
the dust settles on the skin – a plague

of pollen, whole, dense on the ground,
and we understand the shadow of defeat,

a kind of seasoning in the mind that turns
pride into a pathology of doubt – it's easy

to get why those who left pretend these days
not to have ever been there; it is easy

to see why people keep the history a deep
secret; it is a kind of shame, a wash

of shame I understood; it is thick on the ground
like the pollen; it powders the skin,

clogs the nose, grits on your tongue. I was
not falling in love, just finding my face

in the faces moving toward me.

KD

67.

Tim and I are memorising "new" poems
to recite to each other when he goes to bed.
Tonight he's doing Emily Dickinson's
"Jesus thy crucifix" and I am going
for Tennyson's "The Kraken" in which I
admire his use of colons. Memory
is the issue in the house – how it works,
what it does, what it leaves us with.

We are trying to sort American visas.
Years living in Ohio and we still go
through a struggle – mainly to do with
my need for a waiver… proving
the distance between my old ways
and the new. Tim is an American
citizen so for him it's renewal of soil.

I ask him of his memories of Ohio
which he left at two-and-a-half,
being twelve now, and he says: "The big blue
chair near the glass door." That was
when we lived in Mount Vernon, on
E. High Street, snuggled in behind
massive black walnut trees.

He says he remembers the porch
swing on which he swung with me
and his sister, then fourteen and wild.
But mostly he remembers the Kroger
supermarket – being in the cart
and Katherine singing to him,
"Turn around Timbo turn around"

as he looked everywhere but ahead –
Tracy pushing the cart, his sister
so alienated and distanced from all
of us now. And a big bear at the front
of the shop – a model of some sort –
but not bear of Big Bear which he
also remembers, the shop empty

and forlorn. And the women
at the till of the Seventh-Day Adventist
store who called him "Li'l mayn" as he sat
in his pram with "King of the Road"
blazoned across his t-shirt. I ask Tracy
what is indelible for her, those five years,
and she says walking through heavy

snow, heavily pregnant with Tim,
driving through heavy traffic down
to Columbus on the I71, and taking
Katherine to Wiggin Street School
on icy and warm mornings. We
haven't seen Katherine for years
but Tracy says she knows

what *her* strongest memories are;
she knows them to the core of herself:
tapping maple syrup at Sarah's place,
visiting the McBride house (the old
Philander Chase mansion, founder
of Kenyon College), riding home
on scooters, playing Hermione

Granger in the book-club play.
And all of us replay our visits
to the Amish town of Berlin
and the surrounding country –

their constraints something
we understand. My memories
are tied to those of the others,

but the sight of deer through
the window, groundhogs in the fields,
the pileated woodpecker striking
reflections out of car mirrors,
and our walking the Kokosing trail
in snow and summer weather
make the comparisons

and disjunctions I live by
in the here and now. How close
or removed from the rest of what
America is, I can't say, but even
when I memorise Tennyson,
something triggers images of passing
through, temporarily belonging,
but able to translate the chatter

of nuthatches and cardinals
… or sliding, eternally sliding
on black ice, trying to wrestle
the Dodge Neon back into line
on Kenyon Road downhill
just before we met the T
junction with Coshocton
Road and destiny.

JK

68.

The friends with the dead daughter
are not talking to each other.
The silence of years of a well-shaped arrangement,
a kind of détente in mid-battle, fills their sorrow,
and they have forgotten how once
they were the scaffolding for each other,
the finely entwined exoskeleton
that held them together. Their silence
now haunts everything, it smells
rank with long unburied resentments
and blame – and blame is how we
sustain our wounded selves, how we flee
from guilt. I think of such silences,
standing in the soft chill of early morning,
after days in the un-ironic blaze of the Caribbean
and listen, sound after sound, deep into the dark
to find the hum and grumble of traffic,
and I think of the silences that fill
John's mornings there in Australia,
the silences as ancient as the rituals
of survival for humans who have walked
and walked and walked in search of green,
and deep meaning in the open sky,
who have cultivated nightly dreams
of emptiness, a world free of predator
and disease, of a simple gum tree where
a worn-out body can sit and wait
until its breath is full of the starry
clouds hanging over everything.
We desire more than silences, those
yawning spaces between us. I ask Lorna
how long they have lived like that,
as a couple without being a couple,
and she said, *Years*, and I said, *And how?*

And she said, *I did not ask, it felt too*
intrusive, and I said, *I am a writer I suppose*,
and she said *Yes*, and then the silence
grew in the car – filled by the earnest
curse of Steel Pulse, "Chant a psalm a day…"
I know that these are the sorrowful
days of my ordinary life – the small gaps
between trips – where we hold our tongue
so we do not stumble over each other
because whatever rituals we have formed
in absence to fill the absence must not
be disturbed by these brief interims
of presence, and today I catch a flight
to London. We kiss; she says, *Enjoy*;
I say, *Sure*, and then I count the days
ahead, count the things I will miss, and think
of all our arrangements of love, think
of how we repeat the stories our children
tell us, of what Kekeli said last night,
trying to find where sorrow lies in him
at his news of a friend who blew his head off
and was buried by his father, the Anglican priest,
and they had a nice lunch at the Thai place,
he said, though not to me, but to Lorna.
To me he said, *I don't know how to feel.*
Do I cry? I don't know what it means to lose
someone like this, as if it must mean something,
and yet there is this odd fascination, a kind
of pride in being able to say, *My friend,*
he was a cool guy, he blew his head off;
it was ugly. And this is sorrow. Afterwards,
we grow silent, after the theology of things –
how a life of faith cannot be snatched away
by some dark act of desperation, at the last minute;
what cynical evil makes a man construe
holiness as constantly at risk, constantly

in jeopardy of being withheld? Mercy, Jesus!
We are rehearsing the languages of affection,
the languages that we hope we will soon be able
to conjure when the silence is too much;
but for now, I think of my friends, the couple,
sitting in their duplex, looking across
the deep shadows of a Kingston dusk,
trying to find comfort in forgetting,
and how this will never happen.

KD

69. A version of Petrarch's *Rime sparse 189*

Midnight, the dead of winter,
and my ship, laden with lost memories,
sails a rough sea through Scylla and Charybdis
while my lord, my enemy, holds the tiller;

a wicked idea strokes each oar
and seems indifferent to tempest and failure;
a dank, remorseless wind of despair,
desire, and longing, leaves the sail in tatters;

a scornful fog, a weeping rain,
soak and loosen fraying ropes
distorted by ignorance and error.

My familiar, dulcet stars are hidden,
and logic and skill are dead in the waves
such that I despair of reaching the harbour.

JK

70.

The poet in his room will then eat God
                        — Valzhyna Mort

Full-blood Ray says he sees child-snatchers everywhere
and his wife bleeds when the children are stabbed,
the girls, really. He worships the memory
of a peyote high, holding in his arms a bleating lamb

like Christ. Michael, the apostate poet of faith,
quotes Paul badly, as if to rewrite him,
mouthing him as we say in Jamaica, which means
to insult him – the blunt madness. I say eat, drink

and be merry, as a prophet would – something about
Roman poets and their pragmatism. Today all this
is polemical poetry. All these like sheep have given
up, and the tyranny of doubt hovers over all magic.

There is a 5th-Avenue-dressed lawyer who hangs with poets
saying to all, again and again, *Where do you want to be buried?*
We avoid her eyes, though inside we wonder
what you do take with you, we who were born astride the grave.

I wish I could claim restless genius and a wild
imagination, but all this happened one winter night
when the air was funky with the boastfulness of intellectuals
and the food was awful to boot, and yet, there it is: light!

KD

71.

Light here is the devil flames of small fires
burning parallel, then linking when wind-rows
converge on a tree which becomes a torch.
Burning off. The blooding of the sky
as mockery of the fire season gone.
"Necessary" is a confusion the firestarters
play with, and the Firebug below us
has filled the valley with smoke
because filling the valley with smoke
is what he thinks he's supposed to do. Truly,
it's for the hell of it. We are enveloped.

*

Maybe the smoke stirred my insomnia,
irritating at the edge of sleep. I kept repeating
"irony and insomnia", "irony and insomnia",
as if it would be a key to being upright,
to walking the solid if shaky earth.

*

Sleights of Clearing: an aetiology of landdeath in the Wheatbelt

Let the burning-off "accidentally" run the treeline or ride
the trunks of "strays" in the paddock – always a pain to take the tractor
around, though useful markers are rockpiles, admittedly.

Put in a new fence along the road and take out the Long Paddock vegetation
further than necessary, because no one will say a word and there are
more than a few officials out there who will see it as doing them a favour.

Put in a new firebreak three times the width of your usual or what
the law requires at the point where bush sidles up to the fenceline –
bite a little deeper and do a bit more each year and then graze sheep
through, and again and it will soon collapse in on itself. Burn remnants.

Let herbicide mixed a little stronger (oops, slipped) drift and drift.

Take your yearly percentage – what you're "allowed to clear" – and nibble away
at the same patch over ten years and it will upturn laws of diminishing returns.

Cop the fine on the chin – go in at night and bulldoze your inner sanctum
and it will be years anyway before they discover you've got a new paddock
or two carved out of the bush, and it's unlikely anyone will have the balls
to pursue it in court and if they do bother fining you, the returns
on the increased harvest will more than compensate. Just think,
what a legacy for your kids. The farm more profitable. If not forever.

Get your local right-wing member elected. Band together – you can do it!

Claim clearing will increase employment (even if it's only for a few days,
and your new seeding and harvesting plant will cut down "man hours"
anyway, so it's a win-win from your bank balance's point of view).

Ringbark and claim a pathogen struck the heart. Or blame salinity
which just happens to climb, leaping the cleared spaces to your
solitary trees, sheep shade in the paddock – but who's going
to complain about sheep baking in the sun. Seek compensation
for your treeloss and ask for assistance to tackle the salt scalds.
Those who don't make the land work for them are fools
and deserve to have it cut from their hides.

*

Maybe the smoke stirred my insomnia,
irritating at the edge of sleep. I kept repeating
"irony and insomnia", "irony and insomnia"
as if it would be a key to being upright,
to walking the solid if shaky earth.

*

And I thought, embalmed by smoke,
listening to Tracy's uneasy breathing,

the smoke seeping in, that every time
I try to make oneness with the united
states of being, I go through the agony,
the information dump that makes
a nineteenth century narrative
with contemporary collection
methodology. "Irony and insomnia".

I search old files for anything
I might have written during
application for my last US visa
and came up with this
draft of an unpublished
poem (July 2005 files):

Are you now, or have you ever been
unwilling to accept that nation built out of religious persecution
      must persecute to keep itself religious?

Are you now, or have you ever been
unwilling to own a gun, care for a gun, try a gun out
      down the range, brandish a gun in the privacy
      of your bedroom, play Sergeant Fury in front of the mirror,
      shoot an intruder?

Are you now, or have you ever been
unwilling to accumulate: possessions, money, grudges,
      gratitude for the dead animal on the table, skin and bone?

Are you now, or have you ever been
unwilling to have God on your side? God inside? God fully
      gestated then cloned? God at your dinner table? At your
      favourite fast-food restaurant?

Are you now, or have you ever been
unwilling to drive a car, illuminate your house, shop at Walmart
      have your children vaccinated?

Are you now, or have you ever been
unwilling to take your freedom under Democracy? Democratize
       your freedom? Renounce the speaking of French
        though admire the belligerence of Napoleon just a little?

Are you now, or have you ever been
unwilling to call Walt Whitman "Father of Democracy"
       or accept that art and self-publicity
        brought creative writing to universities?

Are you now, or have you ever been
unwilling to die in Iraq, kill in Iraq, liberate Iraq?

Are you now, or have you ever been
unwilling to accept English as the language of loyalty? That Spanish-
       speaking in schools is the civil war of tomorrow?
        That the Civil War is the crucible of modern America?
        That the melting pot means variety in the military?
        That you understand your enemy better
        by having him or her closer to you?
        That Mount Vernon in central Ohio
        is primarily white, Christian, corporate?

Are you now, or have you ever been
unwilling to accept that creationism is better for schools?

Are you now, or have you ever been
unwilling to believe that Hell awaits those who say "yes"?

Are you now, or have you ever been
unwilling to give up the glory of nature for profit?

Are you now, or have you ever been
unwilling to watch the films of Arnold Schwarzenegger?

Are you now, or have you ever been
unwilling to accept that some are more equal than others? That
      the unassimilated need to be kept on a tight leash?

Are you now, or have you ever been
unwilling to confirm that Ted Nugent hunting with a bow is different
      from his having sex with Courtney Love at thirteen?

Are you now, or have you ever been
unwilling to accept that drug companies are different
      from drug pedlars on the street?

Are you now, or have you ever been
unwilling to accept that metaphors are not profitable
      in the way mixed metaphors line silver pockets?

Are you now, or have you ever been
unwilling to respect the drive of those who keep porch flags crisp,
      who say peace comes with strength?

Are you now, or have you ever been
unwilling to let free speech direct the winds of change? That
      "some are more equal than others" was always a many-lane
      highway, or a two-way street with traffic lights?

Are you now, or have you ever been
unwilling to call the wilderness of Alaska "wastes" awaiting
      development?

Are you now, or have you ever been
unwilling to allow that Western Australia has the right to develop,
      to cut back on A Class Nature Reserves? To transform itself into
      the West Coast of the Antipodean American Free Trade Empire?

Are you now, or have you ever been
unwilling to accept that Maralinga fallout bears no connection
      to prospects of clean energy from the new generation

of nuclear reactors? That one was about weapons,
the other about letting you see clearly at night,
watch television, make music without instruments?

Are you now, or have you ever been
unwilling to accept that Philip K. Dick was delusional
that time is moving faster, that it all might have been
just a week ago? That the committee is meeting tomorrow?

Are you now, or have you ever been
unwilling to accept that Ireland is part of the "British Isles", that Cool Britannia
en-flourished the common tongue, that Celt is currency
in the New Europe? That visions and prophecy
are the raucous bird smuggled out of the Kimberley
and kept in an aviary, a conceit of climate change
and missionary zeal: say a Silver-Crowned Friarbird,
or maybe a condor slowly repopulating the Grand Canyon,
or the imaginations of tourists.

             *

And to think, that once when I did sleep, I dreamt
that James Dickey hunted me down and ate me.

JK

72.

(i)

I am hoarse, so much dry talking –
the rituals of language can be
a hike through a sun-dusty field –
after an unexpected meeting
in a gentrified city; the sun
is here now and bodies
are stripped down to the summer
promise. Soon everything will go
blurry with the softness of a folk-
song with such sweet traps
in its melody – how easily the tears
come. I won't say I love this city;
mostly I try to find my footing here
while Oxbridge types resent
the box I put them in, but how
post-colonial is that, Neville?
At some point, even with your fox
fur and your regalia, even with
your cultivated tongue, you
lamented the seduction,
and might have envied me
singing *Light up your spliff*
just a chain or two from the palace.
Well, it is bleary blue here,
an impressionist's take on a waltz,
where people dance on lawns
of pale green and soft light,
where the men dress in black
and women carry their froth of lace
about their frumpy selves –
time to move on, people. Got to run.

(ii)

These tumbling songs we shuttle across
the empty air between us – miles – there
is still nothing in our DNA to read this
speed as anything but magic. We wait
in our own dunghills – these bodies
are ancient as blood, they die
with ordinary predictability – and this,
perhaps, is why we think of poems
as the trace we leave, a kind of marker,
tombs, or perhaps the bones of black
slaves, four of them sacrificed
under the kind ministrations
of a Catholic priest gone rogue,
all the dust, the blood, the ancient
stones. It is easy to stand at the jungle's
edge, stare at the alarm of alien
mountain ranges, and think
that perhaps, here, God's appetites
are dearer, hungry for flesh,
the enchantment of Christ's sacrifice
again and again – this is called
a special sin, a kind of comic
ritual of a speeding creature
walloped each time by surprise.
They buried them at the four foundation
posts, 1521 – the building still stands;
this is the legacy of the blood we bear,
in a cobbled street in Mexico City.

(iii)

I arrive early, ignorant of the city's
way with light. The sun is still
high, a kind of glow that softens

all lines. Too early, I walk to a café.
A woman, her face white
as Russia spewing out the French,
is drunk on all that flirtation, her tongue
heavy on the consonants. The latte
is tepid, grows colder in the cooling
evening air. A man, in black and clean
as if someone washed him and picked
out the clothes for him before
sending him out with warnings,
approaches with the posture
of petition – black man. He asks
for food money, adds, *At least
I was polite*. I quarrel, *Instead of what?
Instead of jumping me?* The rehearsed
logic eludes him. He waits, panicked.
I give him heavy coins. *Food*,
he says like I swear, crosses himself;
it is a false altercation. On the hill
the light turns Herne Hill into a village.
I am arriving as if on horseback;
then I make my way to the musician's
home, modest as an immigrant's
caution. We eat fish, listen to Otis Redding
singing in his sad, sad, meaty voice.

(iv)

They say if I place your
    skull, Neville,
in the soft cup of my
    neck-back,
it would fit as bones
    fit each other,
and cherished there

soaked with my
sweat, I will sleep
   the sleep
of the contented.

(v)

It has been almost four decades since that sense
of impossible good fortune in a girl's
body, open, willing to face me, to draw
into herself the intrusion of my hunger
for her, the thing she read as love, and how
she spoke of love with such ease and knowing,
while we slipped into the circling bass-line
and a voice caressed us and then let us move,
the unquestionable sex of this slow two-step,
the scent of hair, cologne, perfume, sweat,
the deep language of my body trying to read
the friction, every contour of it. I never come
to this thought and not think of you, Neville,
as if loss and desire, and the end of the celibate
are part of the single song of memory. It comes
to me here in this city where you, too, I am sure,
found surprise in the magical, maybe the grace
in the dance, and it is the earnest sense
of a boy who fears death before he can
know the dialect of a woman's desire.
It has been three decades, then, let's say
three, and so now I watch the music
of bodies pairing in the warming city,
how always, at the sweet surface of things,
the dance offers us the safety of desire
ritualized for the music – a soft restraint,
a poem, a sweet music of held flesh.

KD

73.

I have been thinking of rituals – the cost
to foxes, to the flag-waving, souvenir-collecting
subjects. Of dynasties and primogeniture
and the ledgers kept by the greedy. Tomorrow,
on a small island off Java, the Indonesian
government will execute people of the world.
State murder. Vigils have begun before
bullets have been fired. I have been
filling the silence with details. Tennyson's
trances he feared so much, how we measure
our days against news of the deaths of those
with whom we went to school. Or hearing
of the grave illness of an ex-mother in-law...
never really simpatico, but nonetheless,
nonetheless... so long ago. And the small
monuments that compile over days of absence:
    what adds up to our lives, the bits
    we don't tell. Yesterday, walking
alongside the Avon River – no, the Ballardong
River according to a Kickett elder –
Tim and I saw a pair of white-faced herons
converge on the same pool, and a night heron
petrified in broad daylight, hunched on a branch
staring through its own reflection. But the revelation,
was an echidna making its way out of the vegetation
towards a drainpipe where it might take shelter,
being on the edge of a town. All this, and the rare
green huntsman spider – Neosparassus ZZ572 –
on the wall by the front door. All of this,
    and I am caught strangely quiet,
    inarticulate in speaking out... out.

JK

74.

It is not by design, at least not design
I dare be honest about, though,
if asked, I will say I immersed myself
in the questions that have long tickled me:
the outback, the roo, that slim volume,
the novel I read twice at thirteen, and before
the dream could take me, I gave up,
thought – too much sun, too much sand.
But here is that Davidson woman; last
night I watched an actress in a sarong
kill a dog, drag camels across sand,
and that beautiful snowy landscape –
the woman's body without sex,
silhouetted against the blue, her eyes
hungry for a reason. We mourn the dog,
she says, and I have no desire to ask her
now, after the blue of the Indian Ocean,
if she still longs to be far from humans.
Or the long tail-end of that Great Train
Robbery saga, the fugitives turning
Australian so easily. It is how I read
when I was thirteen, growing invisible,
or transparent, until all that remained
was a bodiless head, an imagination
of elegant deception. You always know
that there is a hunger remaining; it is
the thing we call longing or lonesomeness.
When I read of other landscapes,
I was lonesome, and I relished it all,
as I did the deep grotto behind
my primary school that late afternoon,
a year after I had left, standing alone,
filled with the deep belly pain
of desire and daring, the terror
in my body, my kindling palms

rolling, rolling, knowing that something
would be damaged and something would
be opened, and then there it was,
the brokenness of orgasm. This
is my body, I said, this brown
body, this nose, this penis, this pain
inside me, this alarming terrifying
body. Here is how I imagined
Crusoe, then, as a body standing
ahead of me, about to discover me,
about to feel the hand of me, hard,
and the equation was no longer
loveliness. I am watching Australian
dramas, soaps, the green lawns,
the cities, the sweatless bodies,
and most of it seems a familiar
falseness – that is until the grainy pixilated
photos of the thick moustaches, short-shorts,
grinning drunken eyes of the cricketers,
armpits dark with funk, the ground
patchy, something familiar as a war
might be – nothing orderly here,
and I imagine that it does take
the same hallucination of desire
that makes a woman long for weeks
of open plains of sand and scrub,
the deep silence of absence to occupy
a prairie land, to stand stoic
like that old man on my street,
over-baggy sweats, a walking stick,
hair in waves of white, watching
the hired hands making a bed
for tulips – and he sees nothing
but waves and waves of prairie grass,
the Spanglish in the air, like the slight
irritation and discomfort of a fly.
John, at the credits, I think of you,

think of your walks over scrub
and light, of the family browning
to the colour of the earth, and I know
I am half blind to it. It is curious
how today a metaphor offers itself.
Just this morning – the moment
the doctor told me to go, to take
up my accoutrements and walk,
the alarming colours of the street,
the sharpness of newly seen things –
it was as if I was re-seeing the world,
as if this too was a restored film,
and I slowly missed the muting
of my lens-less eyes –
the delayed recognition, the way
edges softened around the world,
and how comforting that was, how
thin everything seemed to me,
how beautiful my days without
the grotesquery of detail. If I come
to you through these elegant poems,
these laments, these quarrels,
these protests, these filtered memories,
perhaps I will find something
of a home, perhaps I will settle
in that surreal instance of a woman
stretched on her back, glowing
with the tender orange of dawn,
while a blued python swims over
her torso – a pristine icon of faith.
Tonight, the lens, like the best poems,
left me dazed with a throbbing ache,
and this, too, is what I have feared,
that suddenly so, without rhyme or reason,
what was promised me in one instance
of illumination, will be taken away.

KD

75.

(i)

Your virtual Australia, Kwame,
might be less virtual than you think –
you know the colonial importations
of a London where the streets were
once lined with the jarrah of the south-
west forests, the ancient trees cut
as slabs by my ancestors, the theft
of the body-parts of "Aborigines"
so men-of-science could dazzle
their colleagues (and the ladies),
broadening the mind of the "centre".
Or how Australia sells itself
to the "rest of the world", the uber
other of non-Australian existence,
which it has been conclusively
proved (scientifically verified)
is out there. When a "black" dies
in custody in the United States,
you know what black deaths
in custody are here. Different
people, different histories, but
to the dwindling white establishment
clinging to their perverse cult
of purity, it's a beacon. When
my brother and I resisted the right-
wing nationalist groups in the 80s,
tearing down their hate posters
and doing more than taking it
on our pacifist chins, we knew
the truth of it. Seen the film
Romper Stomper? The Nazis
might have favoured Brazil,

but the Klan have their followers
here. Written out in the Baz Luhrmann
spectacle that is *AUSTRALIA*,
insiders, never mind outsiders,
struggle to see the wood for the trees,
which is maybe not surprising given
so much of it has turned to woodchip.
Not allowed to say this, but because
I grew up white with darker "white" skin,
I was called "black Irish", whatever
that meant. Armada residue? Storms
off Spain and Portugal, a touch
of Moor? My brother was called
a "White Abo" in the shearing
sheds for years, a term of absolute
hatred and vilification. He was not
ashamed. He rathered it that way.
He knows where his allegiance lies.
This is Australia, Kwame,
and I invite you and Lorna
to "our" place at Jam Tree Gully –
land stolen from the Ballardong people
back in the nineteenth century. We know.
We know. But you'd be welcome here
and we'd show you around. It's our
home, too. Our home on stolen ground.

(ii)

"*Unearthed* is a tangible example that the dead are always with us."
   — Hazel Menehira

Tracy's last book of poetry, *Unearthed*,
is a book of elegies. She has been
surrounded by the dead since
the early passing of her beloved,

older brother. We write out
of a place of genocide, a place
of death. Death speaks out of foliage
and the dead grip the roots of certain trees.
I once wrote a book entitled *A Book
of Rural Disasters* (later renamed *The Hunt*),
which tracked the deaths of farmers and labourers,
of all those who die in the agricultural enterprise –
this feeding the world spectacular. When
we were in Ireland – where we will be
again shortly, the ghosts of our ancestors
grim and unreplete with death, and those
who made it to Australia struggling
to reach where they might go –
I grew angry with death on death
of farmers working with slurry –
cow and pig shit fertiliser brewed
to potency in closed pits, pits that once
opened release a killing gas. I was so disturbed
that I wrote to Irish newspapers and included
this address: another death by slurry:

*

Another death by slurry:
this time a thirty-seven-year-
old man overcome by fumes,
pulled from a slurry pit.

A couple of weeks ago,
a father and his young son:
father survived, son dead.

It knows no borders.
Today's tragedy in Co. Cork.
A fortnight back in Co. Antrim.

The brewing of cowshit
in closed pits, a hydrogen
sulphide chemical weapon,
banned under all other conditions.

But this makes grass grow.
And grass makes silage.
And silage makes cows.
And cows make milk.

It's a basic equation,
a life-death scenario.
Complain of the stench,
and watch the grass grow.

Not all tradition
is good tradition. The usual
ways are habit-forming.

On the verge of summer solstice,
the soft-eyed cows chewing and shitting.
The endless work of fertility.

Another death by slurry:
this time a thirty-seven-year
old man overcome by fumes,
pulled from a slurry pit.

*

This mixture of agitprop and lament
fell between those proverbial planks –
neither poetry nor epistle, a degenerating
rhetorical lyric that leaves
the issue stranded. But death
is death and that's something
many Irish seem gripped by from birth.

Halloween. Absurdity. A wry
laugh at the unfortunate self.
Where do we belong in this,
wanting to lessen the number
of dead, bring all back to life
without a quota, without
a record of who they were
and where they'd been?

JK

76.

There are images that remain,
a patchwork of pieces – the in-between
of that maddening line of time.
I wake up as far from the madness
as dreams are from me, call them
thugs – it is easier – and we know
who is to blame for the tyranny
of the peaceful march, as if
all dignity is found in the body
given to be beaten and dragged,
as if all anger is noble, as if
the broken spine of a Baltimore
man held down for his crimes
does not cause him to shit
himself, and puke, and be all
animal, as animal as the sticky
hands of men who learn to slaughter –
the dirty work of butchering,
of slicing open a gut, breathing
the deep rot of a stomach, feeling
underneath the slippery lumps
of offal to find a cancer, which,
remember, is something quite
rotten, and smells quite rotten
and drips all rotten, and takes
to the worms as easy as days-
old flesh; even the white coat
of the surgeon will smell of blood,
and the hairs in her nose
will cling to the labour of the dead.

(ii)

And why must the anger
be clean? Who says that when
you run into the wide open road,
the bitter burn of gas swirling,
who says that this terror
has a reasonable end? Fling
the stone to confound the void,
reach for the cinder blocks
and hurl. I have no useful
answers. I am sitting in the half-
light of morning; already my body,
even before day break, is weary,
and what I long for is not more
sleep, but a day of emptiness
before me, something akin
to a patient's void of convalescing
in a hospital in a strange country
where you do not speak the language
and the water is heavy with silt,
and the food is salty with brine,
and tomorrow the sun is filling
the green-blue glass of the bay window,
and then leaving it blank as a sky.

(iii)

If I close my eyes I can see it all:
a field that stretches far, further
than my eyes can consume,
and the green is constant,
a bland orderliness. Then I open
my eyes to see emptiness,
and what I feel is the joy
that ends all Kundera novels —

something false and seductive,
a kind of political stasis that says
two bodies fucking is truly
the end of all things – which is not
true, since even that conquers
nothing but the breathless moment
when all thought suspends itself.

(iv)

Islands of tawny grass, a complete
silence between the inexplicable
strips of green: I make this
a metaphor of our art, John;
another – as if we are lacking
in these – this Manet boy, standing,
looking out, a too heavy sword
filling him in the absurd way
of war – how we can never carry
the universe in our hands,
how ridiculously brave we look
awaiting the executioner. I say
we, as if I have stood before
a line of rifles. I have not –
which is why this is all art,
though the terror, I know –
the stomach unfurling itself,
the thighs growing so weak.
Beyond him, on the edge
of the canvas, lies the emptiness.

(v)

Ms. Gay, the renowned novelist,
has to stand often to let blood
flow to her waist – all this flesh

will press down on the capillaries,
she writes, her verdant patches
of suffering in her music. My brown
body will have no respite;
I will be the Commander,
that easy monster with a penchant
for rape, the bogey man
of her Haitian nightmares;
I will be the one on top of her,
and beyond me are the long stretches
of silence. The truth is she has
long decided that it will be
her blue-eyed husband of Mid-western
dignity who will rescue her
from her brutish father,
those black Haitian monsters —
but this is art, anyway, and why
be so political about it? It is not
my fantasy. It is hers. This, too, is our art:
the spaces in between the silence.

Ps. Even when we stop, our throats
burning from overuse, our heads
brimming with doubt — as if we know
that what we have said is noise,
something to fill the space —
we will both stare into open spaces
and long for water, tepid,
gentle, and somehow soothing,
and hope to be the kinds of priests
who can see in this ritual, *shanti*.

KD

77.

Early this morning the Indonesian government executed eight "foreigners".
Some of the victims refused blindfolds and sang as the bullets tore into them.
Rehabilitation is not part of the lexicon of power. Today is a day for grieving.
We walk through the valley of death: shadows of the fallen temples
of Kathmandu about us. Just over there is where I had my epiphany not far
from the top of the world. The dead rise and the living sink. Why?

JK

78.

I admit, now,
my desire for ancient myths,
but not the bloodlessness
of dusty hexameters –
I do not see my broad
nose in the marble and stone –
and though I know
of the split innards
of those ghetto islands
at the under belly of civilization,
I prefer my myths
to smell of what I fear most:
the broken bodies,
the bleeding, the thin
line of yellow shit,
the flies.

John, I know that here
in these songs,
I am rehearsing
Marley's despair –
There ain't no use,
no one can stop them now...
– in that after-season,
his body rotting away,
his face hollow as a saint
waiting for the flame,
his every word alight
with clean suffering
No one can stop them now...

And this is how we survive:
blind to all, deaf to all, drunk to all,
or constantly leaking

from every pore
every bewildering sorrow,
those lasting things,
the elegies of our peace.
I see the bodies ripped,
I see the tents erected still,
I see the secret compacts,
I see the rites of greed,
I see the beheadings,
I see the on-screen flashes –
how disposable our bodies are –
and no one can stop them now...

How then is it that here,
in this garlanded moment,
I find such comfort
in these muddy lines?
These are the clumsy words
of a drunk priest who has exposed
his nakedness to the believers,
and now they pity him,
pity his stammering,
and have lost the mysterious hold
his art had on them,
but every song must fade,
and what is left
will be ash,
and this, too,
is fine.

KD

79.

Where flow from the drain has cut a channel
down to the river, a large echidna is working
towards the opening, nosing aside leaf litter,
searching for food as it goes. A heavy rustling.

The river is still low in this late Autumn,
but we sense the echidna crossed from the far bank,
across a greenish slick to make for subterranean
shelter, the network of pipes beneath the school.

Tim is restless around the scene of his trauma –
where over the grounds he was pursued.
But looking down at the echidna climbing, into
its small eyes where large worlds are drawn in

and negotiated, there's respite. Echidna's are
strong swimmers. Under the flooded gums
we see its quills as both real and metaphoric,
writing mixed messages of darkness, of light.

JK

80.

(i)

In another age the acidic bile in my stomach,
the film of sour discomfort on my tongue,
the dry flaming in my throat and the constant
cough would mean a catastrophe before us.

I will sit on a wooden chair on a floor of white
cedar boards, staring at a sixty-year-old woman,
whose eastern European accent glows from her nose,
and we will sweat, then start to weep, both of us.

(ii)

Someone will write of this moment and call it art,
the poet and the woman in her copious fabric,
her dress covering a body melting into puddles
of salt. No one will say he is the only African.

There is no rum-bar in my past, but there is a line
of memory, a kind of bias I carry in my head,
where everything changed: on one side the chaos
of not comprehending the dull tyranny of desire,

on the other side, this: how, over time, grief
taught my body to melt, and I learned how to sit
in this room, and stare at this woman, discover
so many sordid narratives in her eyes: human again.

(iii)

For days now, I have thought of the calamities
before us – how we are caught inside a deep pot,
barely staying afloat, waiting for the heat, yes, chaos
again, telling ourselves to stay still, to stay still.

I have, in this, learned how to hold my breath
and await, perhaps, the end of the body's war,
counting coins, putting papers right and, on a long
purple night, to walk the stumbled limp of an invalid.

(iv)

Gathering moments, the bleary cloud of sickness,
I will long for an old Sturge Town woman with a vial of weed
steeped for decades in white rum, that potent
embalming sweetness to lay me out.

Then I will long for her hands, to guide my feet
towards the cool water in an enamel pan,
and her saying, *It will be well, baby love, it will*,
and the sleep I will have is monumental as death.

(v)

I rely on the micro narratives of dramas
on television – this is my labour – the kind they tell me
is the design of the bio-powerful. I am in mud,
stepped in so far, that returning is pointless.

The truth is more futuristic, my portable universe
this box of magical understanding – call me wizard,
call me obeah man, call me shaman, call me priest,
if I don't answer, call me shy, call me humble; lie.

(vi)

What we have with us, what we carry in our box
leaves us with no excuse for what we do not know,
except the stuttering cursor, the unsolicited
pop-ups of seduction: they tell us nothing

that we do not know, and everything we think
we desire. We are mapped – the limits of our ignorance,
the sweet spot of our obsessions – and fed to bloating.
Why would we not weep before Marina Abramovich?

(vii)

Yesterday I searched for Negus and found the red-haired
Scotsman screwing the Ethiopian Queen like
King David did with Sheba, or so he thought,
though this was 1778, and afterwards, he stole

the Book of Enoch – and I think, Esther – and search
the name, and arrive at Abyssinia where black faces
carried wisdom. Renoir's "Le Grand" is the revenant,
the antithesis of health, preserved for the pixels.

(viii)

My ignorance stretches like a vast desert
of the unknowing; it has been days, and my cough
has eased, my stomach is settled, and so there is comfort
in what we have wrought here – you say "survival".

Once, Walcott offered that we Caribbean people
have fought to be among the races we fear and hate,
though he never said who they were – the privilege,
I suppose, of the Manichean sweepstakes.

(ix)

That was thirty-five years ago, too soon, I'm told
to crown the prophet. Today, I admit to nothing
but gratitude. You see, I have never sat still
in front of Marina, never stared at her aging eyes,

never felt the welling of sweet lament – knowing,
of course, that I would be cleansed by it.
But I have needed a metaphor for this thing,
John, that we are doing across water and the dying

reefs that have cradled your island from time,
and this is the best I can do – something absurd,
useless as a man, aware of his body, staring
across silence at another, and finding the gap

populated by something of what it means
to be here, still here, and waiting to be there some more.

KD

81. Petrarch's *Rime sparse 22*

For most of the creatures who inhabit the earth,
other than the handful who detest the sun,
the time for working is during the day;
but when the sky blackens and brightens with stars
some head for home and some nestle in the wood
to get what sleep they can before dawn.

And I, from the breaking of beautiful dawn
when night's shadows are shaken-out across earth,
stirring all the creatures of the wood,
never stop longing after the sun;
and at night while watching the flaming stars,
I shed tears and yearn for the day.

When dusk dissolves the shining day,
and this darkness gives life to another dawn,
I gaze longingly upon the cruel stars
that have formed me out of perceptive earth;
and I curse the day on which I first saw the sun
because it reveals a man naked in the wood.

I doubt there ever grazed in any wood
a creature so pitiless, either by night or day,
as she whom I grovel after in shade or sun;
and I don't relent with fresh sleep or dawn,
for though I am flesh and blood of earth
I am driven by a passion that is of the stars.

Before I fuse with you, shining stars,
or collapse into the carnal wood
escaping my body which will be ground earth,
show some pity in her – a single day
could restore years, and before dawn
energise me from the setting sun.

That I were with her from setting sun,
And none see us but the stars
for a single night… and let there be no dawn;
and may she not be transformed into a green wood
to escape my embrace, as with the day
Apollo chased her down here across earth!

But I will be below earth in the withered wood,
and the day will overflow with little stars,
before the sun arrives with such a gentle dawn.

JK

CYCLE TWO

... To There

Illuminations

82.

Purple thistle flower brazen on a single stem after gales
have stripped late flowerings from all other vegetation.
It's a visual extravaganza, a fuck-you in the roar
of a southerly flow riven with hooks and jags.
Ravens swell around the mummified corpse
of their brother, strung from a hazel tree
by the tractor driver who takes up all the laneway
as you walk head-on, old red sandstone bleeding
into the Celtic Sea which makes colour
outside the spectrum. I can see these shades,
these light-plays in effluvium. What do you see?

The Mizen, West Cork, Ireland

JK

83.

I vow to avoid the language of skeletons this season,
once is enough – the first stripping, the neighbour
sneaking over with her mower to clear our yard,
the revelation of yards hidden for long enough
by the leaves. This is not the season of death
for all seasons welcome the dead and dying, but
the wind from the western plains will turn on you,
cut through you, and make you feel like the alien
you are. I admit I imagine myself a Syrian without
a name, waiting for the church of good people
to drop off a coat for the coming winter. Tonight
no one speaks although they know I was once
in Paris and I speak French. Our house is a farm
and sits inside two acres of safety – I watch their tail lights
and wait for the coming storms. I imagine myself,
too, a farmer; I imagine myself fleeing to Jamaica;
I promise that the next time I say *skeleton*,
I will mean bones, fragments of bones in an urn.
I will be discussing where I want my bones to rest.

KD

84.

Did the long walk again today, and found a raven
near its fallen brother – still there, welded.
I shook my feathers in the nor'-westerly – same
as it did when I passed under. Not complaisance.
Register that the ground below the corpse has been
turned over – a small patch of innocuous mud.
I am followed by rooks, hooded crows and jackdaws.
Though the jackdaws aren't much interested. And
cats. Usually, cats out on those narrow, isolated
hedge-clasped ribbons of road run and vanish
into dead bracken when they see me. But today,
one stopped for a long chat. I am not trying to avoid
talking about what's happening across the water,
but rather to focus on the elemental. I went out
lightly dressed, as always, in the sharp cold
and concentrated on heightening my senses:
to experience everything more intensely.
I studied the bare trees closely, I looked for
compromised leaves they'd lost. Starlings
with darkened bills mobbed the sky over
my hesitations, spontaneously generated.
I hoped for sight of an otter with the inrush
of tide against the dark, bloody rocks.
Back in the southwest of Australia,
tens of thousands of hectares are burning
and lives have been lost. Conflagration.

JK

85.

It is the time of compromise; the pain, they say
will never go, and *never* means death, which, in this
new language, is measurable in years, and thus,
strangely bearable in the way that an old song –
Soon I will be done – can be comforting, for it will be
soon, as soon as light takes to fade. But enough
of this morose indulgence; mostly I walk with a limp,
inside the steel light of winter, and *stark* is the word,
a brittle starkness, while all around me is the persistence
of nature. I have wanted to shout calamity and alarm
at the death of the earth, but this too is like *soon*,
which has its own music, and its own healing trick
of the mind. Imagine the great apocalypse,
imagine the dying of the light, imagine the rot
at the edge of oceans, imagine the detritus bobbing
along the warm currents for a thousand miles – sky juice
bags, plastic bottles, Styrofoam boxes, syringes –
the remains of the poor – alighting in mounds on beaches
where different languages are spoken. I have seen it all,
and yet here in the grey of winter, or cocooned
in the resilient riot of green on my island, *soon*
is the distance between each breath, *soon* is the maybe
of a grandchild, *soon* is the void looming next week
or the week after. *Troubles of this world, troubles*
of this world, going home to live with God, going…

KD

86.

I went back to that originating purple thistle
to see if it had finished – it was just hanging on,
barely there, faintly purple. Lashed by two
storms and its own coding for decline and death.
It refreshed me, seeing the shade of it, and looking
back towards the range divvied up by swirls
of cloud. I thought this whole landscape
with its neolithic burrowings, its extruded
copper heart, could be cast in crayon
and charcoal. I am stuck in representations
of what I see – the old red sandstone bruised
with brambles and bracken and furze,
burnt to the bone in some places, annealed
to the picturesque I refuse, maybe deny.
But I've no negativity for what is there,
or even *how* I see. Maybe I am bothered
by the art *most* seem to want: painted houses
poking pointed heads up over the hedges
and stone walls, caught in a rare sun
lancing through. But with *history*. No one
can deny history! A history of aesthetics
dragged breathless out of the dark bogs,
into the glare. So I sketch where I'd usually
take notes. I colour with "duns and browns"
I drag from a poetry not even of here.
It has consequences, these influences
that have cost so much, dragging
colour from land stripped bare.

JK

87.

They say his speech is gone – strokes pummelling
his forty-four year-old body, this seat of rotund
pleasures – nothing from the dark lips that suck
firmly the delicious smoke; "I have so many addictions,
I have started counting only the passing indulgences –
those fleeting one-night stands." I would not have thought
him a man of rolled-up trouser legs, standing in a creek
deep in the forest, letting the sun and green light of the trees
wash him; but these are the things he wants to say he will miss
while laid up in the ICU, the vessels in his neck temperamental
as the swirling winds in the forests near Nairobi.
His eyes have always been louder than his tongue – huge
pools of alarm, ironic terror and biting sarcasm. Why must
every ode be an elegy? Of course, like all our bodies,
his is turning into something else. They will ship
him to Bangalore, and tender hands will test
the efficacy of his veins. I do not want this winter,
do not want to count him among dying things
in the stainless grey of a Nebraska dawn, the ground
covered in ice, the green of yesterday burnt out now.
My father-in-law says, "These days, my eyes see things,
but my brain does not register them; it is not blindness,
just the way in which the slowing of things with age
teach you how preciously this body is made."
He has forty years on Binya, standing in the light
of the bay window in his pyjamas, lime-honey-
and-vinegar tea in hand, staring into the prairie
sky. But he, too, can feel the movement of blood
in his head, he, too, has imagined that moment
of sudden illumination when even the new networks
of vessels invented by the body fail him, as they must.

KD

88.

Where we connect and who we call upon.
Storm Clodagh is ripping the place up –
Australian eucalypt uprooted out front
of Rosewood Cottage, Tim watching
it go down, leaves grasping then lost.
This is a town that stops for funerals
moving slowly through the main street,
shopowners and shoppers watching on
from under the eaves. No one here thinks
a storm will do much, not really,
but it always does. Shutting things down.
Its Atlantic elegies reaching the depths
of life-support. It's all consequences.
Later, we will step gingerly outside
and survey – redraft our impressions
of a zone we slowly grow into, into
vegetable flesh that grows around us
like an irritation that must be smoothed out.
Where else do we come from – bogland
rising as we hold on to the gunwales
of the house, Long Island Bay boiling
in its own blood. I remember a poet
who wrote of Apollinaire and horses
and blood – the seething violence
of loss. When the calm comes back
I don't know what I will remember,
but I know I must speak out, not
be drowned out, not join the silence
that sweeps in when the ordnance fall.
I see outcomes in the shell of my ear.

JK

89.

Already, I tire of the empty chatter about the weather.
The houses in Oklahoma are squat chunky things,
ducked down to survive tornados,
but a thousand quakes fissure the bedrock;
so much oil to be had, so much oil to be had.
Already I tire of the chatter of football –
black bodies colliding into each other.
I do not care. I have learned the dialect
of downs and carries, I keep a record
of the wins and losses – I wear our colours
and return the smiles in the supermarket;
I do not care, I truly do not care, you see.
Already I tire of the talk of police killings,
"Another one who put himself in the position
to be shot in the head." This under breath
from such a nice man, with a neat beard
and a daddy's eyes, and I say nothing;
I am learning the language of invisibility.
I have never retreated into the deep woods,
never escaped into the emptiness of silence;
I crowd my day with the noise of clichés,
and grow fat with deep inertia.
But the snow has finally come and, standing
in the backyard, everything fades into a mute
silence; in this vestige of a wilderness,
I cannot see the boundaries of my civilization.
This is my last retreat, and to these eyes the snow
is white as light unblemished – a kind of dark,
soundless comfort, and this, at least, is something.

KD

90.

There's no respite from weather-talk here
as things are altering so fast. The *frequency*
of storms won't even allow us to retreat
into parts of speech – the land is reshaping.
On a long walk today I was trying to process
the apparent largesse of the Facebook billionaires,
and the fact that they employ less than 50 "black people"
out of a workforce of ten thousand, and about the hegemony
of Ireland with its Celtic-mythology crisis come out
of imperialist crackdown and breakdown and brutal
oppression to diaspora out of – always people
going elsewhere – and *who* comes back in –
those swing-doors jammed one way. It makes
no sense to me from a pluralistic mindset, the joy
of diversity in making life within an imploding
snowdome. Walking, I paused after 10 kilometres
and looked across at the range, and after 20 kilometres
paused to look again. Hear the sound of an excavator
with jackhammer opening wounds in red sandstone,
puffs of white dust rising up over the sodden fields –
the wind is low today though dark red shows
on the forecast chart, a piece of art in its own right,
a mirror of realworld in which aesthetics
is web design, is a template for imparting
good and bad news in the most pleasant
absorbable way. I don't use Facebook –
thought I'd throw that in – and I seriously doubt
the efficacy of art. But I search out illumination
in every exchange of the senses. And the conclusions
we might draw from these. A winter-shedded cow
stuck its head through a stone window to drink of cool water,
both ears yellow-tagged, its eyes fixating on mine
as it lifted. Its head was brilliant,
the rest of its body hidden.

So much myth entrenched
in this. I filter bits to send on,
making no narrative, avoiding even
subplots. Darkness comes early,
but not too early. We rely on it.

JK

91.

It is hurting my head – these days
a round ball; it used to stretch down –
to carry my mind into the quagmire
of the empires of regret and shame
that is race. I am shaving my round head,
which is a ball these days, and we worry
about my son and Facebook, the way he, too,
imagines that the world can see the difference
between the bubbles leading to the speech
above his head, and the sharp arrow alerting
us to the noise of speech – where every aside,
and stumbling thought in search of prudence
is laid out and multiplies. He is broadcasting
his secrets, and we think how easily
anger can turn to something bloody. My friend,
the physicist on a volcano-broken island,
stomps through the blogs like Jeremiah,
and says he is annoyed when the news won't
describe the sound the rifles made in San
Bernardino – so he can tell the calibre.
"No more soft targets," he intones; he
wants to live in Tel-Aviv – no sheltering bread-
fruit trees. What can I say to a prophet?
It hurts my head to calculate the wide open
space a white woman calls *complacence*. A disease
she does not want: "A feeling of smug or uncritical
satisfaction with oneself or one's achievements".
I am not talking about me here; I am
thinking that I want to step out into the cold
air, to cover my ears with my tam, and walk
across the monochrome of a snow-scape,
a rolling body with a ball for a head, listening
to what sounds like a confab of sea gulls
screaming from the trees, almost a thousand

miles from the merest hint of ocean. Is it enough to say
I forgive? I find myself stopping my voice
in mid-protest these days – fatigue washing over me –
and I say, "It's alright, I think I am wasting too
much of your time." And then I walk away,
my head throbbing, longing for the numbing air.

KD

92.

I ask Tim if he's going to memorise
another *Song of Innocence* for our
bedtime reading. He is tired from having
his eyes checked, the correction of a birth
strabismus which has gone into abeyance.
But he probably will. He has that kind
of mind. I am reading him *Finnegans
Wake* — a few pages every night —
with slight deletions! He listens
to the radio to get his sense
of what's what and lives in fear
of violence coming our way.
Of violence coming anyone's way.
All those countries he wants to visit
but can't because they are eaten by killing.

Tim is writing in Arabic script
at the moment and loves all languages
and all peoples and all music. His favourite
music is Chaka with its Yoruba chants —
he knows the issues of violence and identity
at work in the story, the subtleties of Senghor's
poetry, the intricacy of Akin's setting. I'm sure
I have mentioned this interest of Tim's before,
but I do so again today because it's been
a big part of our home discussion. As storm
Desmond closes in — we are on orange and red alert —
I read of the US senate blocking a bill
to stop those on the "no fly list" purchasing
weapons. The arms industry has made
a country consume itself with violence.
Tim is American. He can't understand
why the soil is a place to absorb
the blood of the shot. Nor can I.

I'll tell you something, Kwame,
that has bothered me for almost
fifteen years. I was at a conference
on poetry at the UN in New York
and a group of us were going
on somewhere, and I said
to the editor of a prominent
black American literary journal –
nice guy, we seemed to get on well –
"Where to now, boss?" and all around me
fell silent. I'd been living in the US for a short
time at that point and this colloquialism from rural
Australia, meant in peace and harmony and brotherliness,
had white colleagues muttering under their breaths
and shaking heads. I was bewildered and then I
thought of movies and literature and history
and the word "boss" and projected into it
the irony and distress of Aboriginal usage
of "boss" in Australia and the white bossman
overtones, and the overlay of discourse
on the question that was of friendship
in a society where words are reinvested,
even if context is inverted. Anyway,
I did my best to redress this,
and maybe I could have
but the shuddering whites,
chewing nails and consciences,
made it impossible. I even tried
to explain contexts, place and affection.
On the surface, it worked. But deep down, not,
I know. It haunts me still. But what is worse
is that I know my companion will have likely
long forgotten it as just another slight
in an insensitive ignorant world.
Some would call this
a *faux pas*.

JK

93.

We arrive too early at the soiree. The still sober
guests loiter around. The light is amber,
true, but the glow on skins is alabaster – this before
the rouging of wine and gin – and then the crickets
begin their cacophony of the pundits.
The hosts offer a brimming cup, I sip and feel
the warmth of giddiness – Lorna does not notice,
so I whisper, "Remember, you are driving", as if
we are ever boozers – we the Christian pair.
By nine o'clock I feel to shuck and jive,
while boyish M–, the geologist, with his perfected
shame, apologizes nineteen times
for the sins of his ancestors – the New Orleans
grandfather with his chirping of *nigger*,
the slaveholding Germans and the Missouri
tribe. "Be thankful for John Brown, he was
one of us. Took a white man to bring on
the Civil War; a Midwestern soul, one of us."
He palms my scalp: "How smooth," he says.
And mine is the art of the papal edict:
Go and sin no more. These days I meditate
on the poetry of Christ on the cross,
quoting old poets as clues to a universe.
That "forsake" line was not the end of it all,
but the throwback to a psalm of calamitous
portends.
            The sky is clean for days, so
the geese barking over the neighbourhood
are a comfort – see them in tiny squads,
uneven lines slipping over the blue.
                        John,
this is for you, friend. "Our sins give us shape,
teach us the art of character, how we can
learn righteousness. Of course, most sins

seem trivial in the face of bloodshed,
and soon the word *sin* smacks of a surety
we will never truly have." We are blind men
tapping our way by inches, at least
that is what old Stevens said, and in fragments
he manages this kind of genius, and in this
small snippet, we can find some comfort.
"No more, soirees," I tell my wife, as we
cross Highway 2. "Cyaan tek dis burden
no more. *Eli eli lama sabachthani?*"
You will note, I trust, the irony of my lament.
But of course, but of course, but of course, *bien sûr*.

KD

94.

I have extreme tinnitus.
I have not slept for forty hours.
I expect no absolution. I look
for no absolution. My problem.
My problem, mate. Where there's
no intention... I say, I know. I am
wary of those who try to touch me
outside the proffered hand, the hug.
Last night Tarantino's *Django Unchained*
graced the airways. The indulgence. And
the German co-lead. Touched by Brunhilde.
The love story. Enough to pile the corpses,
collect recompense. And then, alienating
the constabulary, the director of violence
is in front of stop the murder marches.
Absolving? Exonerating? Over-
determining, the guest has his slice,
artful as *his* past — those realist
paintings that move like films.
Or abstracts that hide the sins.
I have extreme tinnitus.
I have not slept for forty hours.
What are we showing here?
This exhibition of our negatives,
overexposure to the gallery?
I look through *your* windows
in a picture you sent to another
and know how you see those bare
winter branches — belonging
and displaced. Like me. Like me,
too. Our confessions and frustrations,
our intimacies and revelations.

JK

95.

... and the eye must burn again and again
through each of its lost moments
until it sees... — W.S. Merwin

But here comes the demagogue, again,
so fully formed he trompes the eye.
I have always hated cartoons for the flat
passion of their antics, but oh the colour
and the noise, and see the plasticity
of his sneer; it is easy to count him out,
but even the least informed student
of the comic knows the magic of multiple
resurrections, the reruns and the reruns,
and the laugh track seducing us into
deep guffaws. Behind the mansion
he has his George Foreman grill,
and he makes steaks for the wife
and kiddies, and wears loose slacks
and loafers, and is the quintessential
good man, with his buddy the negro
millionaire, who brings the wings
and dynamite sauce; this has been
going on for years, the hubris of wealth.
Tomorrow, more for the eyes to see,
and this burning is the blinking red alarm
of glaucoma, the impulse of the body
to close all apertures. I take these drops to trick
the eye, by cooling the muscles inside
my skull, and I shut my eyes, shut my eyes,
but the colours persist their bombardment.
Funny how we miss things lost so long
ago in sudden illuminations. Like today,
I missed the scent of dead things in the bush,
the swarming of flies, boisterous and bullyish

in the heavy heat, the regularity of blood
spilled from falls, stones, misguided blades;
the speed of night, how unequivocal
the darkness was. In those days what burned
the eye was the substance of all things;
and only when we closed our eyes did we dream.

KD

96.

Eyes. One of mine will go eventually –
the sight, or the way of seeing? Theory
as an app. Trite as macula breaking down,
a burnt spot – arc welder – on the retina.
So, I go to the Crawford Art Gallery in Cork
with Tracy to see The Cooper Penrose
Collection again. Two years have elapsed.
I go to see a bird held by the neck – already
dead – to be examined by the protégé,
the heir of Penrose, with his dog alert
and hoping, the boneless patriarch
relaxed between gun and his lady.
The daughter is caught by the bird's
gaze as well. In a different way? But
I don't like descriptions of what's happening
in paintings. I write of paintings but not of what's
happening – because I don't know, because
my eyes are all wrong, and one doesn't
really work properly. Properly Propriety.
I identify with the bird. Of course. But
I twisted off at an angle to stand dumbfounded
before Stella – portrait said to be of "Stella",
"lover of Jonathan Swift", he who likely
had no lover, and hated her less than
the rest of humanity so in turn loved her.
That kind of lover. Never alone with the wit,
Mrs Rebecca Dingley, her friend always
a third party to their conversations? Stella
and Swift and "Stella". But not Vanessa.
Never. Her look? Smug satisfaction,
only talking with gentlemen, never women?
It's not that. It's nothing I can describe.
But maybe the parrot; yet to me
that's no exotica. Not even on estates

in Ireland, not even in a garden of Dublin.
Cotton trade. Plantations. There's just
no getting away from it, is there?
Tim and Tracy finished reading
Jane Eyre aloud yesterday and we
watched the most recent film. Bertha.
Not far away. *Wide Sargasso Sea*
and the booze that sank me for fifteen
years? Me Us You in every painting,
film, book. So Swift hating all humans
still loved Stella and couldn't face her dying.
Gulliver's Travels a place in which love can't
prosper, those islands just off Ceduna,
right near where we stay at Shelly Beach
Caravan Park every time we cross Australia.
I saw Stella there once, keeping a low
profile, talking with women around
a table-tennis table. So I hear we're
going to lose words to a popster?
That Jonathan Swift's Stella could
never now joke that it's "Swiftmas"
without being sued. And she such
a deadly wit. She had a circle.
Mrs. Dingley scoffs at the idea
Swift and she ever married.
And that's the parrot speaking.

JK

97.

There is a cell. Outside, a wilderness,
not wild in the biblical sense,
not a wasteland of tooth and claw,
of blood and gnawed bones, but a garden
where things are allowed to grow,
where pebbles and stones may have
never been nudged, picked up
by hands. Wild in the sense of miles
before a road. In the cell is a cot.
Above the cell is a pane of glass
separating the wilderness from
the cell. The cell smells of linseed
and ink and the fresh funk of a body
still dying in the slow way of flesh.
Each month, the body meditates
on the news. A small tragedy
somewhere in the world. For a month
the body contemplates every angle
of the tragedy until all that is left
is the slipping away. In this cell
all deaths are stories. All births
are myths. All laughter is a drug,
all tears are magical and ordinary
as piss. On its back at night, the body
contemplates the illumination
of the full moon. How the world
is transformed by light! The body
discovers its inadequacy in such
moments. I have never retreated
for my art, except in this way, trying
to climb out of my ego, trying to reduce
all things to a body – a kind of fleshy
thing – and still it is hard to withdraw
from the rituals of id and ego; and anyway,

you came to meet me in this cell,
I in my brown cloak and hood,
dressed for prayer and penitence.
From my window see the winter-
stripped tree, mute light over
the suburbs, a postman
bringing boxes of books. Yesterday
I lived in faith. I ordered books.
Tomorrow is contained in that past,
and I wait for the arrival of books;
I live in constant faith; it is one word.

KD

98.

I know precisely how this poem will end.
Shouldn't I always? Know? How it will end?

Crossing the Irish Sea in *very rough* conditions
I wrote of the swell, not daring an ending.

Today, we visited a town we often visit
when staying in the English fens – St Ives.

The Great Ouse is high there. Tracy took a photo
of a mute swan with a blue sign on a wall above

and the blue took over the photo. The
swan paled. Contrasts. We nearly moved

there once. Behind the scenes. On the fif-
teenth-century bridge there's a tiny chapel

which needs a key, and on its "battlement"
there's a model of Romeo calling across

the fast, wide waters to Juliet up in a shop
"balcony". Double entendres everywhere.

"Romeo, Romeo" reads the sign. 'Tis
the season. And all of that. But I read

Propertius and am planning two versions
to add to our exchange. To re-illuminate

Propertius? The hubris! Cynthia rides
again, only to get dumped into context.

I like how he – Propertius – shifts tone
and approach in Book III, the love-elegy

almost thrown away only to be dredged
up later. The bottom of the Irish Sea,

the River Tiber, The Wash, the Mediterranean,
the Pond. Thinking I know how this will all end,

I can only say that everything I write lives
in scare-quotes. It's not quite how I speak.

JK

99.

Had they been love poems, full of weeping and longing,
with some glorious secret object at their heart – one who
perhaps died young, making the desire almost holy –
I might have excused these awful mutterings. And to think
I made note that these were good pieces – poems I liked.
It was thirty years ago, and I can be forgiven, but the old
diaries are the evidence none of us need that what we think
of as order, a kind of rationale parade of memory,
is a jumble of inadequacy and mediocrity. I was nothing;
I was a philanderer, I was confused, I was earnest,
I was desperate, I was honest, deeply honest when asked,
Do you make poems, and I said then, no, of course not,
for it was true, what I made were ill-formed things, the stammering
someone without language makes. And I repent of my long sighs
at the simpering poets counting their poems, gathering them
in folders, with such varied fonts, their preciousness,
their earnestness. I admit, now, that there is a miracle
I cannot account for, as miracles go, of how we came to this –
these lines that do not make me cringe, this capacity
to speak as if such language was always in my mouth.
Beside the poem, in the margin, the artist uses inks
of a thousand colours to turn these drab arrangements
of letters in their columns and ranks into this luminous
delight, something that will startle every time a leaf is turned.
Perhaps love will come late for me, but that Propertius
was an infant and then he grew out of the madness of lust.
He found out that love is always late, and what he thought
to be youthful pleasure was constantly lagging behind
understanding. I am saying, John, that this echoing
we are attempting may just be our way of trying to bestir
the body with language – every word set after the other,
searching, I think, for a reason to wait for the next;
and this, we know is our art – the first blue of light
in the morning. Truly, I have come to cherish it so much.

KD

100.

A Figurative Essay

   for Marjorie Perloff

What we say is where we say.
What we say is how we say.
What we say is why we say.
What is said fluctuates.

I am wondering why the Bogardus
Social Distance Scale can't work,
but why it can operate as metaphor.
I am thinking over the failure

of the three unities: all place
as disruption, all time as collapsing,
and all action as a set of consequences,
some of which will contradict

intention. Bogardus offered this
cumulative score card, this set
of questions to discern, to map:
As close relatives by marriage

As my close personal friends
As neighbours on the same street
As co-workers in the same occupation
As citizens in my country

As non-citizen visitors in my country
Would exclude from entry into my country.
Blood and soil and rights to spill.
I changed the spelling of "neighbors"

to "neighbours" because of familiarity,
though I lived on & off in Ohio
for many years. The "u" is not part
of Ohioan English. I look for a Roman

poet to work away from, as I have
done with Ovid in Exile, Virgil
in the Underworld, Horace in his
embroilment with praising the emperor.

Patronage. All of us, eternally outside
and unable to belong, wonder
if it's worth throwing our lots in,
trying to join up. I wonder

about that inversion designed
for "white" appeasement and comfort
in Eastwood's *Grand Torino* where
Walt Kowalski (Polish American)

tells the *pretty fly for a white guy*
guy that he wouldn't expect the *black guy
gangbanger stereotypes* to want him
either. This, Marjorie, is where

words *out of context* are deployed
by audiences doing the survey.
We say things when we're tired
and caught off-guard and have been

the victims of concepts, but they
become indelible. The weight
of words. It's why I won't deploy
"denigrate" in this poem,

and why "avant-garde" can be
taken down – shock troops so many
want to be part of without knowing.
I read of Juvenal and the dumping

of the muses – do we look further
than his "Jews", his blame game?
All that cloud worship? Victim,
victimised, victimisation.

The inevitable, where I come from.
Bumping shoulders. Calling out.
On whose land I dwell – damaged,
repairing, calling oneself a custodian

as if waiting will rectify? The fact
of red-capped robins intensifying
a season, my absence when the mistletoe-
bird picks the gelatinous orbit

around a seed, or the wattle-seed
itself – the fruit of the host – ground to flour
in the season of burning. Absence.
And so context shifts. I watch

home via photo essays, I read snippets.
My brother the shearer visits.
The Guru watches over. My mother
photographs. Dzu phones her daughters

in Malaysia. I ask for manuscripts
stored on a shelf to be typed up
for my book with Charmaine –
against mining, *against* COLONIALISM.

I am against what I come out of.
There is no comparison. Is there
juxtaposition? The killing by colour.
Deaths in custody. There is.

Marjorie, you tell me of those last
trains out of Austria and the family
member who went back for *wrong*
reasons. She doesn't deserve.

She didn't deserve. Deserve. Deserve
to serve death. She didn't. Murderers!
Killing fields, its slippages into the montage
of history to dilute down from being

there. As in our cultural allotments
we can't reach across, mis-say but *mean
well*. To absolve themselves some
will come with righteous agendas

to cover their own pain. This is
part of it. *It* – trigger word
of modernity. It. Not you or me
or us, but it. Remember the film?

Conversation transcribed
is a reinvention of tonality,
and even the playing back
of a recording removes

atmospheric context. Clouds.
One has to have been there,
move towards resolution,
rather than use it as a weapon.

A cultural space you are not
part of and cannot be part of?
How to undo, restate. The
repetition of kangaroos in my

Jam Tree Gully work – they are there,
and then shooters come, and they are not.
They and it. The it is deleted. *They*
covers – myriad of sins. Conflation.

You are too inside America
and have now become polarised
in the debate, and thus whatever
you say is going to be played

back against you. Too much
of the debate is centred on making
America great for all, rather
than deconstructing the concept

into parts that show that any
projection of power is going
to bring internal prejudice
and bigotry whilst holding

the carrot of "you can be part of this".
I have seen so many clouds
of late. So many. Whereas (I hear)
Jam Tree Gully suffers from cloudlessness.

What we say is where we say.
What we say is how we say.
What we say is why we say.
What is said fluctuates.

I know what you are saying.
I am away from the original
conversations. I am glad Tarantino
marches against police

violence, the selectivity
of killing. But I know that
his films exploit. I know that
violence as entertainment

is not resistance to violence.
I know that Chuck D is right
regarding Elvis. And that he
is wrong, too. Break binaries;

it is a peaceful act to step
away. I have survived on *stop,
think, act*. When out of control,
I regret speech, writing, metaphor.

Snippets reinvented to suit occasions –
acts disrespectful to a victim's integrity –
the words we have made: body, carcass,
flesh, identity, love-hate (a tattoo), prayer.

It makes it no less a crime
to kill someone who is not "perfect"
(or even far from perfect), and
creating false "saints" diminishes

a cause. *Perfect* etymology. Real person
and real corpse and real consequences
nothing to with "saints" or "sinners",
with theories or art. Brutal fucking reality.

Always peripheral, belonging
to no community, having no centre
of debate, I noted many non-African-American
Americans seem to want *Africa* out

of the African-American equation. "Black
American" is *tolerated* – "American" is the totality
of national identity. Reality deployed.
Here, rivalries over DNA. Patents. Words. *Tolerated*.
　　　　Fear as bunting.

Anita Heiss wrote a poem that goes,
"I am not racist, but…" She has stood
by her identity. What it has cost.
It is not economics. It's presence.

Where you are, I have been – *It* gets down
to brass tacks, thumbscrews, a generic
love of guns, *love of uniforms*, a desperate
desire to hold the Union together

while confederate romanticism
lingers like fumes out of rotting vegetation.
For some. *Summa cum laude*. Tolerance levels.
I am inside and out. Inside out.

Now, I write from the Cambridge fens.
UP NORTH, floods have wiped away –
or sandbagged – belonging. Some locals
will stay resolute, others leave for higher ground.

They will have different backgrounds.
Different origins. Difference. Différance.
I won't edit that out. That's what I mean.
Place is altered – we are all part

of the immensity of the event.
All culpable. And not. Water is blood.
The body politic, the body earth.
"French revolution". "American revolution".

Pat sayings – what we take to suit ourselves.
Or the fire ravaging remnant southern forests.
Or displaced, finding the mass graves
of *ancestors* in Ireland. And yet

part is English too. And even
American. Segments. I who have no nation
but have "country", and not even
that concept is mine. I live on borrowings.

From my exile I see your goodwill,
I despair when people hunt others down.
Outing has killed. Let people speak
in their own terms. Let people speak.
     Silence no one.

What we say is where we say.
What we say is how we say.
What we say is why we say.
What is said changes.

JK

101.

My son does not know it. He sweeps into rooms,
Karl Marx beard, his jacket billowing, his threads hanging

on him with the grace of a hipster, Doc Martens
stomping the ground as if he owns the place. He is the cool

drummer, the intense thinker, binges on films;
loves the dark holiness of the movie house. Of course,

I know he is running from the mundane questions
a man must answer; it is how youth resists its end,

searching for a kind of immunity born of neglect.
Of course, I say I had no such luxuries. Dead fathers

sometimes leave nothing but the enrichment of art,
the kind of thing that starves out the giddy of youth.

But I am not dead yet, and he does not know it,
the thing that began the poem, the thing I have not

said. He is like the monarch in deep sleep while
the cabinet quarrels over his fate as if what is at stake

is the thing that will break them apart. The metaphor
is strained. I mean to say, we his parents are his

cabinet, for this is the role we must take now,
in the wings, suggesting that perhaps he might do such

and such and not do such and such. It amazes me
how, in that inbetween place of manhood and childhood,

it is impossible to know how to approach the sleeping
beast, how he will wake, what things he will mouth off,

and why we care, since, after all, we do feed him. Still, John,
I am allowing this weighty thing hanging over my days:

the appointment with that beautiful man who, I know,
has no idea where he will go, and who lives his days

avoiding the questions that have caught up with him –
to have its way instead of the litany of end of year

disasters. Good God, what are we doing in this world,
where rumours of war and reports of floods and calamities

are the ritualized markers of our hours? It is just as easy
to not think on these things, though early in the morning,

I think of my son's limbs, his lithe body, and I think
that it is quick, it is warm, that we are not preparing

for the sterilized mourning of memorial service,
that we are not testing the depth of the gloom

of our loss. So, yes, this waiting to speak, after Lorna
and I have edgily agreed to find a way to speak to him,

never admitting that it is his sleeping body, and the worry
of it that leaves us prickly, and then silent. I admit, here,

that a part of me is amused by it all; because I know
how absurd it will be in five years when the tyranny of this world

will have set things in place. There is small comfort in humour,
though, but small is something, and I will take it today.

KD

102.

My mum lost track of who I was in my youth as I zig-zagged
across the world, addiction and fury shifting co-ordinates.

Listening to Felix da Housecat and thinking over the empty
nest of a reed warbler seen today at Wicken Fen, I wonder

what set me off on that path of abandonment. As things
gradually came back into focus – thirteen steps

doing much more than metaphor – I laughed & fell
& laughed & fell. In memory, I pass a swamp I once

helped save from annihilation and laugh at my vestigial hubris –
the major road I drive on the compromise. A patch for an area:

the trade-off. But that's way back, too, on the edgy suburbs
of Perth before they'd been made full suburbs. I mix

my registers, my sequencing. I live non-sequiturs. And now
in Cambridge – again, again – I admire the growth

of Wicken Fen, the work put into extending a nature
reserve back into farming land that had taken the fen

in the first place. The finches and blue tits,
bearded tit and "scarce" marsh harrier, the lodes

replete and eel-thick. The making of new horizons.
But… but… the paradox: huge wheels of water birds

rising to occlude the low winter sun. And shots fired.
And more shots. For on the edge of the reserve

a lake used by hunters – the distress of birds
not being able to land where they'd settled, lifted

with each blast impacting water and light, the new
horizons themselves. The senselessness.

I need my disorders, but not like this. I want
to stay focused. An "untouched" peat layer below.

JK

103.

On the third day, at three-forty-two in the afternoon,
the prairie sun starkly illuminates the world against
the hard shell of snow. The blue crystal air, a windless cold,
crisps everything. The clipped BBC voice in my ear
rehearses with evenhanded calm the bloodlettings of a year
that's slipping away, all those white bodies broken
so that a citizen-witness can say, "It was as I have seen
it on television in Third World countries, a war zone."
And no one speaks the names of the broken
black bodies curled around a kerosene stove, empty sandals
and charred shirts strewn over the exploded market,
chickens, goats, and slouching dogs calmly picking
at the remains. I hear over the BBC voice
the loud barking of the Canada geese,
this time more urgent than three days before.
And only when I see the sky crowded with a hundred
frantic birds arrayed in the grand v of migration
do I realize that the small squadrons languidly crossing
the sky three days before, in well-spaced out teams
of four and five, only then do I know that they were
the *avant-garde*, the scouts, the advance team.
And only when we see the mob consuming our days
do we know what we have missed all along.
I have no idea what this means, this strange
revelation on the edge of a new year, except that what
I feel now, this hunger inside me, a kind of anticipation,
this mawing of my heart, is the evidence of what
has long departed – old news. There is this small matter
of faith: "This can preach," the old black evangelists say.
"I go to prepare a place…" We should call this, John,
"The Gospel of the Migrating Geese". But that chance
has passed, too. The sky is empty now, the way
a street empties, leaving the static hum of absence
in its wake after the soldiers have passed through.

KD

104.

The white militias are heeding the ranchers' calls
in Oregon, Kwame. The patriarch and his boys
have taken over a wildlife refuge and declared
liberty for white folk – miners, hunters, and ranchers.
And maybe "their" women. But that's complex.
They say they are not terrorists, that they will not
fire first. Locals are terrified, with a few notable
exceptions. They have their arsenal on display.
It's a nutshell. And the arsonists who burnt
space to cover their deer-slaughter have their
own agenda. But still, across the divide, a calling
to *all* frontiers folk who know what a gun can do.
I have received a package from Nigeria containing
a literary magazine edited by my friend Biola Irele.
His next issue features more poems I have written
to Nigeria. He has spent much time in America.
He visited Kenyon. I met him in Cambridge, England.
He has helped make a new university. I think we should
offer some of what we're doing to him, "his" journal.
This is relevant. The BBC has different arms –
it spans the world. It speaks selectively to audience.
Its policy migrates. It is a rare jungle bird being
wiped out by oil interests willing to… well, you know.
A friend questioned my use of the word "exile"
for myself. I said I would explain sometime.
There are many inflections of the word and concept.
Those who have shot at me, those who have poisoned
my water in the distant past, those who have made
it clear the fate that awaits. Those who drove our son
from school beating him and ranting Nazi creeds
reconstituted in "the weird melancholy" of the white bush.
These are the clues for us to work with – to unpick
the riddle, to make a new Exeter book without an
accent that doesn't exist anywhere in the world.

JK

105.

I have been searching the sky these last few days
as if looking for an ending. Today, there was barking,
yet the sky was empty. It was a single creature
barking, and I searched the sky hoping to find
just one last goose, a kind of arrière-garde, the one
who straggles in case anyone is hurt or has lost
its way. But the sky was empty. Still, I blame my sight,
for the dog kept looking up, yanking on the leash
as if she, too, wanted to follow. In my head, these days,
I am constructing plots – sometimes I am infested
with the art of fiction. I grow fatigued by poetry.
And while I find little solace in fiction, I still find
it healthy for my brain to pile plot upon plot, to hear
voices quarrelling in my head, and I pretend to myself
to take notes. Here is one: there is a character
in a series I have been watching for a week – a kind
of binge on betrayal. For days my body carries
that strange sickness of someone who has hurt
others, relentlessly merciless; and my body is waiting
for the retribution all stories should have, but it never comes,
and each day, I list her betrayals – they are legion.
Then in the final scene of the final episode, she falls
into a coma, while the world festers with resentment.
This is a curious cruelty. I believe that people who make
such art are the geniuses who advise politicians.
They know how to make plots filled with desire
and longing, but the healing never occurs, and this
is a kind of art. Your man Flanagan from Tasmania
tried to say something like that, something about
how poets, too, can be brutal, something about how
we are not one thing, we are many, and we can make
beauty, and we can make the ugliness of life. I am
supposed to agree, but I know that for all my
self-deprecation about the poet – "Oh we are not special,

we are just the one's who learned the craft". I know
there is more, a kind of capacity for regret, for lamentation,
for human feeling. *History is the history of humans*.
The poet who murders millions is a failed poet,
and maybe it is true that all poets are failed oracles,
but some failures are more abject than others.
It is not just language, it is more than that,
it's a way of seeing, and something happens to us.
It's as if we are born with a holy defect, a sixth finger or toe,
a caul, a wound made in our forming. I will deny
this if asked, but will say it here: "This. That which we do.
It is sacred." We are not arrowing ahead. We are
the dizzy stragglers, picking up the jetsam
of the thunderous horde. And that is fine, too,
for when we get there (and we will, make no mistake),
we will have stitched such lovely elegies to keep us
honest in whatever stickless land we light upon.

KD

106.

Yes, poets are too often brutal. I am writing an elegy
for a town that has been brutalised by fire. The
town of Yarloop where I lived thirty years ago
and visited barely six months ago was "wiped
from the map" two days ago by a brutal
fire-front feeding on the brutal air of a brutalised
climate. The fire still rages out of control.
Is it irony that Yarloop was a milling town,
the tall hardwoods falling to its dizzying blade?
Is it irony that it was a railway town, its workshops
full of skill and pride and waiting out the Depression?
Is it irony a great Aboriginal poet grew up there?
Is it irony the irrigated paddocks burnt
to their veins and the water stopped coming,
and the town was left desperate and vulnerable?
All those animals and birds caught by the flames,
spotting so far ahead they made new erosions
to join up with? Traffic diverted. Firefighters
worn and blistered and too overwhelmed
to join the dots. There's no time for metaphysics
or ecology or politics or hope. Just get the job done.
Maybe you have to have grown up there to know
how a greenie and a right-wing nationalist
can forget what the other bloke thinks
and dig in, stand in front of the flames.
It's no ritual of fire and earth and water and air.
There's no time for fucking around. No art. No poetry.
It's brutal. As brutal as poets and poetry.
More towns are threatened. Forests have been
vaporised and ashed. Evacuees retreat
from one town to another to evacuate
again. Two old men in Yarloop were
not evacuated and their remains
have been discovered in the pyre.
I am writing an elegy. Elegies

are brutal with loss. I weep
for the death of a layer of land
I know. I weep for all loss. And now
we wait for snow to come to Tübingen
where we have just arrived. Ensconcing,
settling, projecting to the burning place
we come from, the heat rays deflected back.
"Like spring here," says a local. It should be frozen.
We wait for the snow to come to the medieval town.
The town of Alzheimer's and the botanist
the fuchsia was named for, introduced to Ireland
and woven into hedges and a flower symbol
of Cork. The flower late. Their bells ringing
fire fire. The burning. The brutal brutal burning.
And not eight days ago we couldn't travel
to Brontë country on the Yorkshire moors
because flooding had broken
the back of infrastructure. We
look for resilience, we long
for resilience, to know we could
and can do it too. It's brutal talking
about the weather. A pastime. An obsession.
This is an elegy, too. This is what I write
from where I am. I am no less there.
Last year and the year before
we were close to flames.
You never forget.
You want it to stop.
Even seeds opened by fire
know there'll be little to grow
towards, little to celebrate
on opening. And this is more
than human intuition, the river
Neckar running close to here
around an island, our isolation.

JK

107.

My world is so flat these days that I have found
no vantage point to see the turn of a river, the way
it cuts through a landscape. When I was in school,

I learnt of oxbow lakes, the mystery of erosion,
the reshaping of the earth by river flow, as if these things
happened in a year. I was in love with contour lines,

reading the depth of a valley on the flat surface
of a chart, by the thin isolines on a map. I thought I knew
the mystery of the earth, then, and perhaps I did.

My world is flat, my days are flat; I see the earth
as a series of roadways that repeat themselves each day;
this is a comfort to me with my weak eyes, it is true.

I have learned the roads by heart, and though the dark
mutes all the edges of things, I can find my way home,
heart throbbing, yes, but believing always in miracles.

Today I said I want to know the contours of my words;
I said this as a writer would, having that deep
knowing that all my art is a study in what I have failed

to do. I understand the attraction of the monk's
silence; everything I speak becomes a lie after
it is spoken; everything I reach for becomes

an indulgence in the ego of things, and I move
in crowds longing to be silent as a monk. It is daft
to want to be holy by escaping from the dirt

of our humanity, but waking up here on Oregon's
coast, I relish the holiness of my silence before
the cacophony of talk among the crowds. John,

I read from our poems some nights ago, and so I did
not do my flashy dance, and I felt so naked on the stage,
which made me think of how intimate our music

has been. A woman, afterwards, came up and said,
"Are you okay, so much talk of dying." In that moment,
I was thankful for our sacred hovel of language, how holy

it is to speak of geese migrating, of houses burning,
of the wounds of our present and past selves, of the raw
foolishness of our art, with the broken beauty of words.

I will come back now to the flat surface of things,
the absence of contour lines in my world, for you know
as I do, that it is a sort of lie. But these illuminations,

they are my new cartography. I will say no more
of it. I dread the canker of the ego, the insincerity
of confession. I am grateful, John, for these shelters of trying.

KD

108.

They *are* full of death, Kwame, but what isn't?
What we do. Where we go. How we make of it.
But today is Tim's thirteenth birthday and we
are celebrating it with the music of Toumani
and Sidiki of Mali – the notes of the kora coming
through the apartment – and the Afro-Cuban
All Stars lined up next, to be followed by
music from Guinea Bissau and South Africa,
the White Stripes' first album, and three volumes
of Telemann. His class at school in Tübingen
sang Happy Birthday in German, French and English.
When he was in first year primary in the wheatbelt
he chose to dress up as a boy from Mali
for their dress-up day. We also gave him
a book on Tanzania. He absorbs but takes
none of the world. He talks with it, doesn't
take its speech. He listens. Snow is falling,
and while the snow falls, I hope. The hills
gather in with their forests, and I watch
a grey heron fly through this poem. Soon
I will walk out of this room and cross
the old town to home under the castle.
It will weigh heavily on me, but not the snow
which I will dust from my coat. The salted
ground will still be slippery and I will think
of the white agony of salt in the wheatbelt.
Of the blinding heat. Of the despair
which is here also in so many ways.
How can it not be? But many in their
comfort don't see it – the rug from beneath
their feet, the mat at the door smudged
with ice and mud and muck. A slurry.

JK

109.
for CD Wright

The body of a woman is marked by the wisdom
of the living and the dead. The rituals of catastrophe
and renewal are written across her flesh;
it is not that there is mystery here – that is fear –
instead it is the thing we most covet as sucklings,
the terrible eloquence of her body's genius.

She flies above mountains; there are grand narratives
in the peaks and valleys of Chile. This after Glenna
returned renewed, despite the year of mourning her body's
betrayal – the cancer. She returned in her aquamarine
scarf and her pastel-red fish-eye glasses, to the tawny
desert, and wrote reams and reams of true music.
"At last," she said. "I have tapped into the eighty-year-old
sap of my body, and see what brilliant colours I can make."

In the morning, the handsome husband turns to face the soft
light of Providence – the familiar scents and shadows
of home – after weeks away; they return deep in the winter
to the comforts. Beside him, the CD dies,
a clot rising through her veins, deep beneath her skin,
settles in her heart, her white hair is tidily graceful
on the pillow. How does death creep on you like this? What
dreams can keep you so cocooned, as if under snow,
that the world can explode around you so silently?
She was kind to me in China, where we walked beside the lake
where poets have scratched their lives out for centuries,
and I felt, in that moment, a part of consuming history.

In London, one summer, my father sat in a stranger's
armchair, smoking cigarettes, in shorts – his thin
legs, veined and muscular. Thrombosis, they said,
something secret in his veins. This would be our summer,

waiting for the clot to dissolve itself into a dew,
while we made new friends, ate bangers and eggs,
wondering about the language of death and abandonment.
This was 1976. He did not die. His heart stayed intact,
he was only fifty then. The betrayal was six years later,
his body falling down stairs, his heart, still intact,
pumping and pumping and then not:
the last redundancy. He was fifty-six then. I count
the years. I am fifty-three now. Here is the light.

There is snow in the air, a kind of hanging
mess of dust; everything looks like shadow
in relief. I am searching the haze for a sudden
flame of colour. This morning, a poor poem ended
with the alarming genius of a line – a poem:
"Flash of my white nightgown in our dark yard".*
It arrests me for its reverse image – the way
it undoes the white and black of things in my world.

It is as if everything I consider today
is about the way our bodies begin to move in the morning,
the undressing and dressing, the vulnerability
of our naked selves, and the way that the memory
of dying is a kind of music in the air, brittle,
crisp. Someone, I say, will write the gospel
of our time: the billionaires who make all desire
all protest seem like a futility of the tragically
redundant. The truth will be told in small
slivers of light, lines in poems. I do believe this.

*From "Of Shock" by Nicole Cooley

KD

110.

On Blake's Illustration of "Dante in the Empyrean Drinking at the River of Light"
(Paradise, Canto 30)
and IMM CD Wright

"The genesis of an ending"
          — CD Wright

Drink deep of the river of light,
CD, your lines of the quotidian
wrought deep, of breakdown

and reconstitution. We wrestle
with sunlight, unravel our paradox.
Snow is rarer and then comes harsh —

bend of leaf under the weight.
I note today, climbing the castle hill
brazen over Tübingen, snow heavier

but vanishing before it connects
with skin. Touch? A fade-out of breath
I cannot catch. I thank you for cleaning

my black jacket doused in conversation
and metonym, the three of us talking
the blurred edges of planet over the table.

Forrest, the empyrean is intoxicating,
though reminds me of amethysts which
ward off headiness. Veins of amethysts.

Exquisite geodes seen in museums
and gem shops and in the earth opening
up to take all light into darkness.

It's everywhere. The setting up a terrain-
map, a paracosm to make a personal
authenticity where history shakes

the very presence, eats even into
the flour-grading system circa 1934.
You would both have picked that.

CD, in your voice is an awareness that elegy
can't be written away from the ecology
that imposes, that surrounds the writing.

Child and foliage, herbs and earth apples,
cloud 9, special *affects*, downtime, upwardly
mobile endgame – I can tell from your poems

that all such allusions would come
to you in the updraft, the saturation.
I am far from our wheatbelt home

where I would have written you
a different leave-taking, but I speak
from within the orbuculum: please,
    drink deep of the river of light.

JK

111.

I talk. I eat. I talk. I eat.
The brilliant folks in their scarves
scoff at the idiocy of those like me
who consume television belly first,
with no true desire for wisdom
or intellectual critique – no nothing
of the sort, were I to be honest,
were I to be talking and talking –
just the numbing distraction of story.
I feel no smarter to say that this
hunger for accumulating tales,
repeated again and again with blunt
familiarity, is as old as blood, as old
as a fossilized lump of stool deep
inside a cave. I eat. I talk. I eat.
I welcome the rituals of silence
that snows me over, hours and hours
of a heart throbbing and then settling
inside the circles of tragedy and comedy.
Here, I am renewed; I do not form
words, thoughts, such things
that negotiate the complexities
of emotion. This morning I regret
my petulant outburst – a child in need
of attention, but too crippled to form
the need in words. This morning I rub my head.
It is smooth from shaving, and the feel
of my heavy hand, pressing into
the soft contours of my skull is a comfort.
This morning I stare out into the white
cold of my street where even the cars
have been muted by the buffer of snow.
I plan to walk in the brittle air, my
ankle aflame with the pain

I have not been able to be rid of
despite weeks of gruelling therapy.
What I am saying is that I talk
too much, and there is something
wholly absurd about how that mist
of condensing air that hangs for an instant
before me on long walks is soon
left in my wake, and then it falls,
in brittle crystals to the snow and ice;
and this is my daily orgy of words,
so many words, so many words,
vanishing in my wake, and all that
remains is a kind of shadow, a mood.
I eat. I talk. I eat. I talk. I eat.
I read a manuscript called "Fossil" –
such a beautiful title. I think to steal it,
to put it to better use, to begin a book
with a very stark arrangement of words
describing this archeological find:
a tidy fat worm of fossilized stool
at the far end of a cave, followed
by a well-researched listing of the instruments
used to collect and date the thing.
Then I will self-deprecate about the envy
I feel for that squatting cave-squatter,
who could never know what a universe
of history she might have left there
against the wall, far enough from
the rot of that old air. See? Everything in me
is limping: my tongue, and my brain,
and the ways I navigate love and the politics
of what we do to each other, our skins,
our histories, our fears. Everything
I do these days becomes this business
of trying to place weight on my ankle
and finding it giving way, a surprise,

really, despite all the warnings.
And this metaphor, which we must leave
like this, is limping into the cold street.
Still, the grand silence, which is not death
at all, stretching ahead, is kind of lovely,
so I ginger my way over the crunch and skid.

KD

112.

The long tunnel beneath the Schloss
and its accompanying buildings –
the highground of control and vigilance –
is open-ended but still cave-like.
From Old Town to the Neckar
which Hölderlin watched over
for forty plus years, writing "late" skerricks
I think more brilliant than others do,
grinning and thanking, just across
the road from the "facility" that treated
his madness in 1806/7 (a plaque says so).
His tower a cave where he ate frugally,
watched over by the carpenter and his wife.
Alone, yearning for his lost love. It had
all gone kaput, and the strains of a classical
world remade the place in the curves
of his turret. History notes and nurtures
disturbance, so I reject it as a discipline;
it is too archivally accommodating.
There was the article in the local
newspaper about the ex-mayor
who revelled in being an SS officer
and responsible for the deportation
of Jews in Belgrade to the death camps.
He'd been a dentist. Local history
echoing like the frozen rungs
in the artificial lake. It is warming
fast now, the cold blip on the radar.
And I read of the Shot Show near
Las Vegas and the acres of acres
of weaponry and the salivating
and drooling and the fact of Walmart's
selling the most weapons of any
outlet in the country. A history

of supermarkets and strip malls.
And that reflex word, "ammo",
the grammar of "liberty" and the "bring
them on" mentality. Technology,
history, kill thy neighbour, *history*.
Is this love is this love is this love?

JK

113.

My daughter, her afro weighed down
by wet snow, sighs our sigh, says, "It is
beautiful, here, when everything is covered
with snow – beautiful!" She means in the bland
browning of spring, the wariness returns,
and we feel like aliens. For a day and night,
I welcome the light off the snow; the roads
are cushioned by the banking, and we all
slow down to a polite crawl, as if we know
the treachery beneath. Deep into
the night, a man calls me who has never
called me, and though he is always loose,
I recognize something needy in his voice;
as if we once quarrelled and never reconciled:
"I remember you, Kwame, as being more
entertaining. You had a sense of humour."
I am doing dishes, I say, which means why
call me, now? He offers me some Rumi, some Blake,
and three sorts of jokes:
"A fat comedian says he loves
the South 'cause everybody is fat in the South, and they
eat cement mix for breakfast." It is a grits
joke, he explains.
               "I hate those southerners," he says,
as a kind of preamble for a joke, then like a drunk man,
grows flustered, as if he wonders if I love the South
since he knew me in the South. Then he thinks
(for I can hear him thinking) that maybe
saying "The South" is like forgetting that he wants
to mean white southerners, so that he and I could
be one. And I do the dishes. So he continues
like a tipsy man, though I can't say he is drinking,
but can say he is a sad poet. "They think
that Jesus is in the Confederate Flag. I hate them.

That is the worst thing in the world! …
Nobody was at the beautiful Blake exhibit;
eight million people in New York City,
and I was alone." I offer a kindness about New York:
"You guys are loyal to Donald Trump. That
worries me more."

                                I can hear the ice crackling outside
while he waits, and then he offers his concern
for my humourlessness, which is a kindness.
I know that I am growing old, and so is he,
and so I think that both of us are sheltered inside
blizzards, and even poetry does not bring comfort.
Then, at last, a joke about Robert Burns, something about
the Queen mother, Scottish soldiers wounded
for King and country, a hospital, and the punch-line
in hopeless Scottish tartan-face, "It is the burn unit,
m'am." So I chuckle.
This is the year of our Lord, 2016;
everything this month is how it all begins;
and he says farewell, and for a moment,
I sit, and listen to the winter against my window.
For auld lang syne, my jo,
for auld lang syne,
we'll tak' a cup o' kindness yet,
for auld lang syne.

And surely ye'll be your pint-stoup!
and surely I'll be mine!
And we'll tak' a cup o' kindness yet,
for auld lang syne.

KD

114.

Poem-Review of a Film

I was asked to watch De Heer's movie
Charlie's Country by a German film
distributor and director. To give feedback.
I know De Heer's other films and have wanted
to see this film for some time. I commented:
This is a significant film for a number of reasons.
Firstly, David Gulpilil's acting is first-rate. In fact,
it would be impossible to better it. One of the best
sustained roles I've seen in years – his gestures,
eyelines, and patience in conveying something
beyond speech is wonderful. Secondly, its sense
of "country" (in the Yolngu sense of the word), is superb.
Thirdly, though some have criticised it for showing
"whites" in a stereotypical way, I think it's a fair
representation in terms of what many (especially
in "community") indigenous Australians experience
of all-too-many "whites". There are a few scenes
I don't personally like (the buffalo strapped
to the car bonnet), but that's the way of it. Over-
all, it deals with place and belonging
in an incredibly sensitive, sometimes ironic,
and always honest way. The script was co-written
by De-Heer (Dutch Australian) and Gulpilil,
and it works. It is a slow, still film with a lot
of fixed camera shots, but that shows a respect
for place and time in keeping with Charlie's connection
with his country, and his search for ongoing connection
in the face of colonial white culture. A couple
of telling lines from the script:

Cop: "You can't sit around on the grass all day.
    Times have changed."

217

Charlie: "No they haven't. You're still trying
            to change our culture to your bastard culture."

The use of Yolngu language is essential and vital
and culturally powerful as a resistance against English.
In fact, the use of the name "Charlie" in some ways
disrespectful – his Yolngu name should be used.
"Charlie" is the easy name for whites who patronise
and dismiss and generally fail to comprehend.
The positive conclusion to the film is *not* sentimental
but affirming. It's the only option other than loss
and destruction. It is the responsible and necessary
outcome. And interestingly, in such an ending,
it is also a statement about art and its cultural
value and relevance. And in this film there's
a merging of place and language and art
and the spirits of ancestors (calling to them,
searching for them) that reaches deep
from one culture to another to illuminate.

JK

115.

How you can tell
from a black and white shot
the cool of a man,

I do not know;

the cigarette dangling
the soft eyes
the gaze

the way his wrist,
muscle strong from
whipping the ball
to fine leg,

bends into an almost ball.

Kekeli tweets the image –
"the original" he tags.
My son never met my father

and, like me, he is now finding him
in the stories of my mother
in the laughter of my sisters
in the legends of our making
in the genius of his art
in the smell of Kingston,
all that chaos and dust.

"The original" he tags,
and I tag back, "Ah Neville,
Triple OG."

To think we have made a home
in Babylon, to think that without
the salvation of jazz, my father
would have rolled the bombs
himself, to think I have found

in this wide landscape
narratives he would never write,
to think my son
will meet him now
and imagine his own counter-revolution,
a kind of legacy of questions;
this is art.

The snow is melting,
and the city grows ugly again;
and each morning
I listen to history,
short and punchy,
the litany of what will stay
and what will be forgotten.

On a trip into the Carolinas,
hunting for a school to teach,
young Dubois found a doomed village
behind a blue mountain
and at the white superintendent's home
they shared a meal;
ruled by the veil
they ate first
while Dubois watched,
then he ate next
alone.

One day we will sit on the gravestones
of our ancestors, my son and I,
and I will tell him this story,
and we will listen
to the ghosts deliberations
and wait for the music of truth.

KD

116.

Here is no place I can be,
no place I can call up,
no place that offers
more than its own
self-directed history,
a history saturated
in the death-cult of its
cartography. Two days
ago, housing – empty housing –
being prepared for refugees
was grenaded. Frequently,
the bloody fire of burning houses
making pictures out of night.
The far right are mobilising.
This is Germany. History
is more than history.
Ghosts of ghosts.
Residue is fallout –
killing the Black Forest,
fuelling industry *and* outdoors –
it underwrites *die freie Natur*.
Omnipresent, clandestine,
outside textbooks.
We speak with those
of the left here who will
oppose a reinvigorated right,
who will open their doors
and their place, who will make place
more than *Volk*, more than Teutonic
Knights and Caspar David Friedrich
bringing classical ruins into the ambit
of a national sensibility. They
are gentle people who love
the lyric but are suspicious

of what it carries in its lulling,
in its beguiling strains. They
will not let the arsonists
fuel a growing hate. These
burnings, their precedent –
this moment, this place.

JK

117

First along South 77th, where it turns into a maze
of illogical design, then up Stevens Ridge Road,
all tree-full Ashbrook, East on West Shore Drive,
along South 84th, down the curl of Cheney Ridge,
then the debris-festooned Amelia Drive, with the geese-
glutted lake with its No Trespassers signs;
eventually, South 78th Street, and back home again.
The ankle has not collapsed – this is my hood,
these are the coordinates of my daily walk,
three miles of meditative ordinariness,
the body limping along, deep breaths;
the world assumes the pulse of this body,
and here I welcome the coincidence of thought,
and imagine that where that spark
of meaning happens inside the brain
lies the matter of poetry, of what poetry
might be made of. As if the round-headed
Dubois, with his tidy whiskers and elegant
style, might encounter the landed New England
Frost, freshly alit from England and the looming war.
It is true that ten years separated these musings,
but this is The Veil, is it not? It is how the fence
is made, not the use of stone or timber,
not the politeness of the divisions we make
despite the unruly branches of apple trees
dropping their overripe fruit on ground
covering roots that cross the limits of our
properties, not the tidy boxes we make
of our world. Those are the musings of Frost.
With Dubois, the matter is brutish, to build
a fence one must own that which the fence
limits, and for those who have nothing, whether
elves or negroes, serfs of slaves, New Englander or no,
a fence is a prison, an annoying interruption

of the long stretch of deception. Open
Georgia lands in the black belt are nothing
but the bounty denied the labourer. We all know
the language of division, the rituals of the civilized,
but how easily a fence becomes the synecdoche
of our decomposing civilities. Why summarize,
why not lay the cards out, making room
from the breath of meter: then side by side
another new art is made: present, urgent
and lamentably luminous to our time.

I think I never before quite realized
the place of the Fence in civilization.
This is the Land of the Unfenced,
where crouch on either hand
scores of ugly one-room cabins,
cheerless and dirty. Here lies
the Negro problem in its naked dirt
and penury. And here are no fences.
But now and then the crisscross rails
or straight palings break into view,
and then we know a touch of culture is near.
. . . . . .
And those over yonder, why should they build
fences on the rack-rented land?
It will only increase their rent.

— W.E.B Dubois, 1903

Why do they make good neighbours? Isn't it where there are cows? But here there
are no cows. Before I built a wall I'd ask to know what I was walling in or walling
out, and to whom I was like to give offence. "Something there is that doesn't
love a wall, that wants it down." I could say "Elves" to him, but it's not elves
exactly, and I'd rather he said it for himself.

— Robert Frost, 1914

KD

118.

Wallace Stevens wanted "order out of chaos",
to see a fence gather in the force of Harvard Yard,
his earliest *Advocate* journalism, his harmonious
utterance to his peers. I have spent years pulling
down fences and writing about what's come
of such actions. And where a fence was forced
on us, I've tried to make it temporary or porous.
Fences across the wheatbelt keep animals in,
humans out. On the strand of barbed wire
running the horizon, tufts of sheep wool
and roo fur. At Jam Tree Gully, I short-circuited
a complete electric fence that the previous
"owner" had kept fully charged and eager.
At night, I hear the ghosts of shocked horses.

Stevens desired a "point of concentration"
which this rambling walk through text
would deny him. But he wouldn't
likely have cared what happened to
Whadjuk and Ballardong and Yamaji
peoples' lines of movement, of being,
when severed by survey and gunfire.
Different tales told by lengths of wire
drawn from the same machine.

But even fences free up different
meanings, implications. I don't feel
I am ever in or out, even when the State
constrained me in its vicious little cells,
"the hold on our imagination which
it is gradually losing" exercise yard?

And then there's Assange in the Ecuadorian
Embassy. All those assurances of non-refoulement,

225

as we hear a jet was waiting to take
Edward Snowden, inevitably, to the US
should he touch down in Denmark.
And the refugees an Australian gunboat
sent back to Sri Lanka; to change the law
to prevent international reckoning within
the fences of government self-interest.

I hear singing as I write, singing bursting
out of a church across the river Ammer.
It is melodious and rises above the church's –
unusually, for here – flattish roof. It is song
tapping into strands of being I don't know.
They are singing to bust out of bricks
in Tübingen. I don't know, I just don't know
what to make of it, what to do with context.
A fence I have half-made for myself.

JK

119.

There must come the necessary despisings and hatreds of these savage half-men,
this unclean canaille of the world — these dogs of men. All through the world
this gospel is preaching. It has its literature, it has its priests, it has its secret
propaganda and above all — it pays!... There's the rub —it pays.
— W.E.B. Dubois, 1920

for Ted Kooser

I have collapsed two histories of arrival
into this alien landscape of wide fields,
big skies, and the lurking history of slaughter,
circling wagons, horse hoofs, and dust.
Even now I cannot shake off the clean
ethics of Hollywood from the language
of prairie history without the blunt
force of art: how corpses smell after
four days in the sun; how babies
left hungry vomit green bile and turn
to bones; how the sorrow and numb
despair enters the body's cells,
multiplying like a cancer from generation
to generation. And the truth is
these two collapsed histories
must be read through the filter
of the imperial anthem, the modern
white man's dogma of inventing
a race because it pays, sweet lord,
it pays. I think it was a snow-heavy
March morning, the campus empty
of students, when I met the spry old
poet, tender-eyed and gracious in everything,
who told me of the morning he had spent
mending the fences about his acreages,
deep in snow, under a brilliant sun,

227

gloved, pulling wires, digging deep
into ice, hauling timber, a kind of dogged
craft – the satisfaction came in the retelling –
and the view of that long unbroken line
across the stretch of uninterrupted snow,
the drift covering every trace of his effort,
leaving these elegant lines, even, going on
and on in a way a poet would call
stanzas, vanishing in the wide whiteness
of sky and land. Softly, softly, he spoke,
of the labour and the art, and I listen
with no understanding of the craft
of it, but fully seeing the end of it,
the gleam in his eyes for having
made it all, and having told it all,
so that a fence becomes everything
it has to be in that small moment,
a studied art. It may have been a year
after or it may have been a dream,
but I stood before a screen against
a wide wall, and the colours were blue
and white and sharp red of the truck,
and for hours I stared at the steady recording
of the making of a fence; no faces,
just the hands and the body of a man
in jeans and plaid shirt, yellow gloves
digging, pulling, dragging, nailing,
mending the fence, the camera not
moving, the sky barely reshaping itself
above it all, and the fence coming together.
I thought of the poet, of the coming of snow,
and I thought of myself standing outside
this world, and thinking of it as strange.
The poet lives with the calm of a man
at ease with memory. Perhaps, he, too
looks out over the white land and thinks

of what the discourse of deeds and treaties
has done to bodies that carry those cells
multiplying and multiplying their despair
and their wounds, and he, too,
grows weary of thinking of what might
have been. Memory carries its own price,
and the art of the American imagination
is the capacity to forget, to bully the body
into starting again: a field covered in snow;
mending fences by treating each log, each
bundle of wire as if it were just invented.
Such is the art of hegemony and holiness.
Providence is a cynic's comfort. What might
have been is an abstraction only if dreams
do not wound us even more deeply
than the lash. Someone stumbled
at line fifteen, and the rest is the blinding
of a blizzard. This is a shame; it is how,
I suppose, we erect our fences. But how
do I argue against the old manifest destiny,
the evidence of the triumphant
and the defeated? And, ah, here is why
Cecil Rhodes still strides over Oriel
College, whispering to the battered children
of his empire, "See? It pays, it pays, it pays!"

KD

120.

I walked out into the "rural" today
and for all its sins I felt connected.
Buzzards in a freshly ploughed field.
The telescopic eyes of the old man
watching our every step, the sharp
line of path and forest. *Privat!* Those
demarcation lines between public
and private space, and still the wintering
animals in their restraints. And looking
into the rare blue sky, I found no source
and wondered what gives astronauts
the right to pontificate on the future
of the "human race". Space race. Arms
race. These old moonwalkers, these
guys who were military to their core,
these evangelists of colonisation
eyeing off the redplanet – *our*
two world empire. Walking again,
I interpolate a language of EVAs
to test bare waters. All those "resources"
Buzz would rather focus on conquest.
The glitterati of cars parked at nodal
points, drivers and passengers
setting off to embrace the open
spaces. Make the trek. Dogs
at their heels.

JK

121.
for Glenna Luschei

In the hills above Carpinteria, on a avocado ranch,
there is perched an elegant home where a poet
retreats among the collected history of her ancestors,
war-broken adventurers, people who built
with the vision of generations to come – the shouts
of the dying, the concussion of bombs slowly
fading in the grand whispering of the Pacific.
Again I ask why I am here, and I have the only
answer God allows me: to listen. Art
tells of his years in the forties as a shrimper
in the underbelly of Texas, of how, when deep
fog would blind them, no visibility beyond
the prow, a white blackness consuming all,
the wives and mothers would drive the trucks
to the beachhead and begin the music of sirens,
a tattoo of horn blasts to pull them to safe
harbour, every deep silence between each
bleat, a kind of holiness, and then, as if
gifted with divination, they would know
when to open up the lights of the trucks,
so that the lanterns would cut through
the fog, bringing them home. I ask him
how did they know when, and he said softly,
Oh, they knew, they always knew, and always
we arrived safely, our boats heavy with
all we needed. I write this tidy lyric
in Glenna's guest book, and at brunch
the next day, she says, without warning,
"I will keep blowing the horn, Kwame,
that's what I will do." She is eighty-four,
and finds it amusing when she has lost
her keys – *Oh they will show up*, she giggles,
and the birds, she knows, will adore

that garish twenty-dollar, yard-sale
bird house, with its medieval turrets,
she has brought to the ranch. Some
people make family of strangers, like
poets turn the mundane into lyric beauty,
and I leave southern California
for the snow of Nebraska repeating
the names of her family – Tom, Yasmin,
Andrew, and lithe brilliant Linda –
as if I am on the edge of the sea, tapping
out on the horn, the secret Morse Code
she remembers from another century
in Iowa, the language she knew to be hidden
there, the language of nations and nations
of strangers arriving safely despite the heavy fog.

KD

122.

What kind of end does the wind demon
out of ancient Mesopotamia intend for us,
wings up, sharp-featured, genitals
encased in armour? Out of a river city
in a seething hot country, the empire
shaky at its edges, impregnable within.
Deserts, date palms, mirages. Camels.
It could be the interior of Australia.

What kind of end does the wind demon
out of ancient Mesopotamia intend for us?
Encased in glass up in the castle, glowering
in a stone room with massive oak beams.
It was windy last night, so much so the rain
blurred the castle into rumour. It was eerie.
It and we were defamiliarised. What voice
did I catch on the harsh easterly?

What kind of end does the wind demon
out of ancient Mesopotamia intend for us?
At Jam Tree Gully, the hot easterly tinders
the eucalypts and we live in fear. Not fear
of its difference, of its personal habits,
inherited rituals, but its monomania.
But few demons are anything but obsessive.
They are interested in passing through
with maximum impact, to wipe us all out.

What kind of end does the wind demon
out of ancient Mesopotamia intend for us,
taken from its resting place, face down
in the dust, riled through constraint
to break free, shatter the impasse?
Harbinger. Obviously. But behind its

remorseless features, its piercing eyes,
its rage, I detected – I detect – a deep
desire for peace and quiet. A stillness.

JK

123.

It does not stop snowing despite this arrival
in Kingston; I must not let myself relax
in the cool February; alertness is all. After all,
this is the city of multiple murders, and this
island has seen such rituals of slaughter.
The dark inside of the Institute of Jamaica
is cool, yet somehow it has kept preserved
the ledgers of hangings, the calm commands
of that Governor Eyre, who cut his eye teeth
in Australia, where they say he showed
tact for the Aboriginals, but here
in Jamaica, the bodies of black people
rising in protest, were layered in the ground,
captured, chopped to ribbons by Maroons
and black militia, while the governor counted
the dead – as if in this he was bringing peace.
500 executed, shade or no shade; one thousand
flogged, women raped. I am alert though,
for the stomach for blood has settled in us;
this year, only, fourteen hundred murdered.
How beautiful is this island early at dawn,
how tender are its greens, how ital are the souls
that meet you with embrace and laughter.
John, one day, we will share notes on the legacy
of our nations in the making of us. My great-great
grandfather carved out the acreages ceded to him,
after Sligoville, the first of the villages
for the newly freed, and while we have no deed,
we have the bones in the soil, a lineage so old
it recalls West Africa as one recalls the lullabies
of birth; and somehow, in the middle of that century,
Bongo Jerry's Muma Queenie and Muma Queen Muddah,
quartered in their palaces, unleash the making
of dread binghy dread, of Garvey, of Drummond

with his trombone lamenting the neurosis of our souls.
"We are all mad," Freddy Hickling says. "It is why
we have no language for madness; it is why we
have planted our wounds on the bent head
of Don D and his laconic horn; as if by his
diabolic blade breaking skin, we too might
live." I will leave for the winter tomorrow,
for the white of that city; and my body will
grow alert to the world around me.

KD

124

This is why I have no nation, Kwame.
I have communities which allow me
to chat, to pass through, and I have
stretches and patches of dirt and rock
I feel attuned to, and I send tendrils
out and am entangled in the tendrils
of the world's foliage, but I follow
no constitution and swear no allegiance
to flag or articles of collective ownership.
I respect the tribes that make up humanity.
I respect the cultures and subcultures,
I respect the animals and plants, the air.
When Eyre crossed Australia, with Wylie
keeping him alive, he took all the glory.
We drive the Eyre Highway across Australia
regularly. The Eyre-Wylie Highway.
But it's the gibber plain and bluebush,
not the stretch of road or rail, that tell
me what's what. When rabbits made
their way across the vast plain,
chewing their way west, it was
the bluebush they conversed with,
and themselves. And the moon flayed
across the floor of a long dead ocean;
this is why I have no nation, Kwame.
The only one open to me was prised
open, gouged out, but nothing was seen.
All the items of existence collected
and filed away in the databanks
of Europe illuminated no one, nothing.
Just yawning, aching gaps. So, I pine
for "home". I receive photos from the Guru
who looks over Jam Tree Gully while
we're overseas. We see a tree fallen

across the distant neighbour's long
driveway, fallen from one side
over the asphalt strip, and over
the divide onto "our" side of the land.
We don't know him well, but we've
been neighbours for eight years.
When we left, he was being treated
for cancer. The tree, felled by a chiselling
easterly after being worked over at the base
by termites, looks like it's been down
for a while. This might suggest.
We might conclude. Suppose.
That things have taken a turn
for the worse, that our neighbour
has not been able to return to his
home perched on the wall of the valley.
We can read an image. We know the vulnerability
of this dry place, even though a thread of green grass
runs down a bank – summer storm-rains brief
and furious, then cut off by the oxyacetylene summer.
This is why I have no nation, Kwame.
And this is why I read your anguish
at the brutality of *then* tearing apart *now*,
the falsehoods of allotting to history
what we suppose, what we conclude.
Drawn from the evidence. Search
the night sky, Kwame, and you'll
find what murderers and killers
and sufferers and victims have found
before. And it is painful, and bereft.
And then it is gone. And sometimes
it won't come back. It can't. It just can't.
This is why I have no nation, Kwame.

JK

125.

I

My song is the Bellevue Sonata,
a ska romp through the delicious
schizophrenia of the tack and boom
of the ska rhythm section
and the loose breathfulness of the bone
transporting a heart to tears.
"Without the music, without
the music…" breaks in the throat
of Bongo Jerry, frenzied dread,
arrested by the heart of the moment,
the illumination of knowing,
"This rass country woulda rass
to hell!" This is how an ancient
warrior breaks into a new wisdom,
the muscle of his supreme compassion,
despite the amassed dead – and
still counting. And the view from
Belleview is a new view; they do
not corral them into the holding
pen, do not anymore offer us
the assurance that the fence
is our marker, the border that keeps
us back from madness. No, these
days, the psychiatrist says, they
are – we are amongst ourselves – we are
all mad to rass, and we must heal
ourselves, learn the pathology
of our fear. Love is this earth's
mission, despite the amassed dead.

II

No one whispers to you – and by *you*
I mean *me* in the way we try to make
distance between the subject of death
and the fact of our confessions –
that ahead is shit and the cleaning
of shit, that ahead is a body
settled in shit, that all love
will be the art of cleaning
the shit of our history while
humming together the suffering
of Job. No one whispers to you
that ahead is a mind softly
transported, leaving those
left to goad, tolerate and coax
with the imagination's task
of seeing a person so fully
formed vanish slowly, slowly;
no one tells you that after the shit
and the hands wiping away
the dead skin on living skin,
after the deep crucible
of their departure – the soul
screaming out of all orifices –
the state will arrive with its
clipboards and clipped tongues,
and usher you out, accused
of not loving enough, even if
not in so many words, though
you know that those are the words.
No one tells you there will
be nights of shit, and dawns
of shit, and yes there will be,
too, the secrets of two people
caught in the vulnerable place

of ministration; the moment
of complete transportation
when hands wash feet, when
the cleansed and the cleaner
are broken by love, so exacting,
so fatiguing, so wearying.

III

And either I'm nobody, or I'm a nation —
The bludgeon that was used to break
us, to scatter us, to turn our rituals
into the ghoulishness of their nightmares;
the truncheon they used to expunge
from us memory of song and voice,
that same thing that makes our poets
stand in open fields and ask,
"Where were you, our gods, while
we called out in the belly of the beast?"
It had a name, it was called nation,
it was called manifest, it was called
destiny. And so, I become nobody,
and though the equation is false,
there are no garments suitable
for this time; the old wineskins
are rotting in the corner, and I have
been wearing their livery, stitching
in a new language. And so I am either
nobody, or am the stone flung
to confound the void, I am a nation;
I am an invented nation, I am
a tribe in search of memory.
This is the cause of a sound colonial
education, and I envy you your constitution
of a borderless earth. But we who had
and it was taken from us, so that we had
nothing, cannot look askance at the tenuous
promise of nation.

IV
                    Unsteady as someone
who has spent months at sea, I recover
slowly from the upheaval of travel; my
body is complaining: I faint, vomit, roll,
and then sleep. Outside the winter is calm,
no snow, but the sheets of ice cover
the curbsides, and the light is a stain
over everything. Were we to continue this,
I could speak of thistles and the purple
of spring blooms, I could rehearse the colour
of our beginnings which, much like everything
that has happened to me over the last two
days, seems like a dream. I am not even sure
where my keys are, where my trousers are,
where my favourite black shirt is hidden.
But it is still midwinter, and what we have
is the persistence of language, you, then me,
then you, then me, across time, across worlds,
while the rituals of slaughter and desire
continue to fuel this world of ours. Reliable,
it is true, and a comfort. It could have
stopped suddenly; in the interim, people
have died, and in books and films, I have
seen the ways in which rituals end;
and even as I lie, face down in my own
vomit, my mind trying to work out
why this numbing of limbs, as if I could
not recall a dream or a critical thought,
I imagined the silence that would follow
between us, you waiting for the next poem,
and then accepting that where things end
is where things end, and in this way
our art, like our lives, like your good
neighbour, both end and continue.
This is a kind of comfort, too, friendship
and its persistence in memory and art, not so?

KD

ABOUT THE AUTHORS

Kwame Dawes is the author of over thirty books, and is widely recognised as one of the Caribbean's leading authors. He is Glenna Luschei Editor of *Prairie Schooner* and a Chancellor's Professor of English at the University of Nebraska. His latest book from Peepal Tree Press is *Wheels*, his eighteenth book of poems. He was born in Ghana, grew up in Jamaica and has lived most of his adult life in the USA.

John Kinsella's many books of poetry include *Armour* (Picador, 2010), *Jam Tree Gully* (WW Norton, 2012) and *Drowning in Wheat: Selected Poems* (Picador, 2016). He has published work in all genres and across a few of them as well, and collaborated with many artists, composers, writers and poets. He is a Fellow of Churchill College, Cambridge University, and Professor of Literature and Sustainability at Curtin University in Western Australia.